MAIN THING SERIES

LEADER'S GUIDE

NO TURNING BACK

15

SMALL

GROUP

STUDIES

ON

FOLLOWING

JESUS

JEFF KINLEY

David C. Cook Publishing Co.
Elgin, Illinois/Paris, Ontario

GREAT GROUPS
The Main Thing Series
No Turning Back Leader's Guide
© 1994 David C. Cook Publishing Co.

Published by David C. Cook Publishing Co.
850 N. Grove Ave. Elgin, IL 60120
Cable address: DCCOOK
Edited by Sharon Stultz and Lorraine Triggs
Cover and interior design: Jeff Sharpton, PAZ Design Group
Cover illustration: Ken Cuffe
Printed in U.S.A.

ISBN: 0-7814-5111-6

TABLE OF Contents

Great Stuff about *Great Groups!*

Welcome to *Great Groups*—a new concept in youth ministry resources from David C. Cook.

Great Groups is a three-tiered series of studies created for high schoolers and young adults who are at various stages of spiritual development. The three tiers—designed to move young people from being casual about Christianity to becoming committed followers of Jesus Christ—look like this:

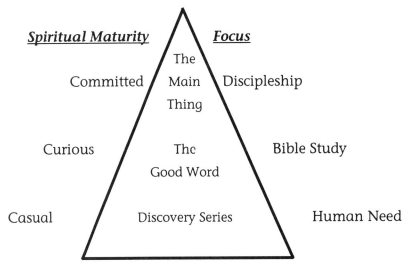

Great Groups was created because:

• Not all young people are at the same stage of spiritual development;

• Intentional ministry is needed to guide people toward greater spiritual commitment;

• Real life change is possible through studying the Bible individually and discussing it together in small groups;

• Many young people are ready to lead discussion groups, so these studies encourage peer leadership;

• No two small groups are the same, so these studies pay attention to group dynamics.

Discovery Series—entry-level studies for seekers and those who've grown up in the church, but who may not have a complete understanding of what it means to be a Christian. These studies help people discover who they are from God's perspective and how that can make a difference in every area of their lives. The *Discovery Series* assumes group members have little or no Bible background. Minimal advance preparation needed.

The Good Word—inductive studies for those who are curious about what the Bible really says. These studies help young people develop lifelong Bible study skills that will challenge them to feed themselves from Scripture. *The Good Word* series assumes group members have little or some Bible background. Moderate advance preparation needed.

The Main Thing—discipleship studies for those who want to be followers of Jesus Christ. These studies will challenge group members to take their faith seriously. *The Main Thing* series assumes group members have some or extensive Bible background. Thorough advance preparation needed.

FOREWORD

One of the praise songs we sing at our student conferences talks about not being "casual Christians." But believe me, they're everywhere.

Casual Christians play the game . . . and many of them play it well. Church is where they go to be seen, not to worship the Lord Jesus Christ. Youth groups are where they go to check out the babes and hunks, not where they go to learn what the Word of God says.

But I don't want to come across as such a downer. Because I know there are many, many teenagers who live their Christian lives with passion and commitment. Casual Christians they aren't.

This book, *No Turning Back*, is a great tool for teenagers who are serious about living the Christian life. It talks about going all out, being sold out. It's a how-to guide—how to take seriously their walk with God.

Too many folks trash American teenagers, and tell them that they aren't smart enough or disciplined enough to learn and live the heavy stuff. I just don't buy that.

That's why students can benefit from this book. It will challenge them to be everything they can be as Christians. It doesn't assume a teenager can only be a casual Christian.

So, let's get into it. Your group can handle it. And everyone can learn from it.

Dawson McAllister

INTRODUCTION

Dear Friend,

I have a T-shirt that says, "The main thing is to keep the main thing the main thing." This book is designed to do just that—to keep a young person's relationship with Jesus Christ the main thing in his or her life. After all, that is what being a Christian is all about.

Unfortunately, too many Christians are just getting by. Their Bible studies have become boring, dull, and routine. As a result, their lives are no different than anyone else's. What this world needs are some people who are sold out to Jesus Christ—people who dare to make a difference for Him.

If you want your young people to be all they can be for Christ, then *The Main Thing* series is for your group! It will challenge group members to push their walk with God to the limit, to seek God's best, and to be nothing but their best for Him. It will give them the tools to live for Christ every day.

So grab a Bible and a pen, and dig into God's Word. But watch out! Once your group begins these studies, there is *No Turning Back!*

Jeff Kinley

How to Use This Bible Study

What Materials Will You Need?

To get started you will need a Bible (we used the New International Version), this leader's guide, a corresponding disciple's journal, a pencil or pen, and if you'd like, a notebook.

In order to lead the study properly, you will need to work through the questions in the disciple's journal along with familiarizing yourself with the information and questions in this leader's guide. Not all questions from the journal are reprinted in the leader's guide, so you will need both the journal and the guide.

Why a Small Group Bible Study?

Jesus believed in small group ministry. Though He spoke often to large crowds, the majority of Jesus' time and teaching was spent with just twelve men. To large crowds He spoke primarily about salvation. But to His small group, the topic was discipleship—how to know and follow Him.

The Bible says Jesus chose these men that "they might be with him" (Mark 3:14). This is the heart of small group ministry—time together sharing our lives and God's Word with one another. Jesus chose this approach to ministry because He knew it would make the greatest impact in their lives. And apparently it worked because you and I are the result of that impact on His small group. This is what Paul meant in his letter to young Timothy—"And the things you have heard me say in the presence of many witnesses entrust to reliable men who will also be qualified to teach others" (II Timothy 2:2).

So why a small group? Three reasons:

1. Intimacy—In a small group, you are free to be yourself, to get personal and to grow close to one another.

2. Influence—In a small group, you can influence a few key people in a powerful way, and at the same time be held accountable by those whom you love.

3. Insight—In a small group, you not only learn from your own discoveries, but also from the insights of others.

Isn't that all we need?

What Kind of Bible Study Is This?

This is a Bible study series designed to "wear out" your Bible. In other words, it gets you into God's Word. It is you and your Bible, one-on-one. It is for you when you want to get everything you can out of the Bible. By the time you finish this book, your Bible should feel like a baseball glove at the end of the season—well worn and comfortable in your hand. In fact, Week 3 will teach you how to get more out of reading and studying your Bible.

Your group members will get to know their Bibles better by looking up verses, cross-referencing, thinking about what they have read, and brainstorming ways to make God's truth real in their daily lives. As you come to different passages of Scripture, the disciple's journal asks questions that help your group members discover what Scripture says, what it means, and how to apply it. They will gain a greater knowledge of God's Word along with a deeper understanding of how to practically live it out. They will write in their journals and make notes in their Bibles as well—underlining, circling, highlighting. As they commit to this process, the Bible will come alive. They will begin reading God's Word in living color. The result—no more boring Bible studies.

But the greatest benefit of this kind of study is that, together, you will come face-to-face with God Himself. God speaks to us through His Word. And every time we study the Bible, we are spending time with Him. What could be more important than that? The outcome of this is that you grow closer to God and stronger in your faith. As you grow, your love for Christ will too, along with your motivation to serve Him.

Isn't that what we all want?

Who Leads the Bible Study?

Anyone in the group can lead, provided he or she is willing to do a little extra preparation beforehand. The good news is that you don't have to be a youth pastor, adult, Bible expert, or eloquent teacher. With the tips, suggestions, and insights found in this leader's guide, anyone can confidently lead this study. The leader's guide will not only help you understand the passages being studied, but will also give you the tools needed to help other group members discover the truth for themselves. Instead of coming across as a know-it-all, you will be more like a quarterback—a fellow teammate who points the way. This will enable you to make it easier for people in the group to share what they have learned during their private study time.

Don't be afraid if someone misses the point on a certain question or comes up with an off-the-wall comment. Instead of labeling the answer as "wrong," direct attention back to the verse. Let God's Word be the final authority. Don't allow the group to get sidetracked or argue. While some debate can be healthy, it is best to stick to the topic you are discussing.

The exciting thing about leading this way is that everyone gets the opportunity to discuss what they are learning. It requires them to think about what they have studied. It gives them the chance to bounce their thoughts off others and to grow from their friends' insights. It is fellowship at its best!

What Version of the Bible Should the Group Use?

The Scripture printed in the disciple's journal is the New International Version. This version is recommended for use in the group. For the most part, it is best when everyone is using the same version of the Bible. However, sometimes having another translation available helps to bring out the meaning of a verse more clearly. But the important thing is that each student have his or her own Bible.

The Format

The study for *No Turning Back* (and each study in *The Main Thing* series) breaks down into three five-week units. Each of these units is an important part of each book, so it is best to study the book in its entirety. However, if you are limited because of time, you could focus on just one unit of five chapters.

You also need to decide as a group how long each study time will be. You should allow a minimum of forty minutes for the study itself plus five to ten minutes of prayer.

Here is a suggested format of a meeting, plus some suggested times.

1 Getting Started (10-15 minutes)

One of the most important parts of your time together. You can use this time to welcome new people to the group, encourage people to mingle, and then get into the frame of mind to discuss the study for the week.

Start on time. This shows you respect your group's commitment to be there. Take a few minutes at the beginning of your group time to catch up with each other. Discipleship must take place in the context of relationships. Ask group members how they are doing and what has been happening in their lives over the past week. Any special announcements could be given at this time as well. But though this is an important time, don't allow it to derail you from getting into the study. Keep it short.

Have a word of prayer before you launch into the study. This is essential because it gets the group into a mindset to learn and it lets everyone know you are dependent on the Lord to teach you.

To be specific, here is how the time is allotted:

Housekeeping (3-5 minutes)

This is the place for announcements (for example, a change in the meeting location or a schedule change) and other housekeeping tasks. Keep it short and sweet.

Icebreaking (5-10 minutes)

For the first few weeks, this section has lighthearted activities to enjoy. These activities will help people feel that the group is a safe place for sharing nonthreatening things. In later weeks, the activities become more serious and lead to deeper sharing.

Opening (5 minutes)

The group can choose to sing or not; however, some song titles are suggested. Do open in prayer. If you absolutely panic about leading in prayer, take advantage of the prayers and litanies we provide. It is not unspiritual to read a prayer—but truly pray it. Don't just rattle it off.

2 Bible Study (40-60 minutes)

A. Focus (Introduction, 3-5 minutes)

This short transition time allows you to use an activity or introductory questions found in the leader's guide. Give the group a brief overview of what you will be studying during your time together. Point out two or three things you will learn together as a result of that day's study. Whet their appetite by pointing out one or two practical benefits they will receive from studying the chapter.

B. Dig In (Observation and Interpretation, 30-40 minutes)

This is the very heart of your small group time. It is the time when each group member has a Bible and disciple's journal open in front of him or her. Expect each group member to have completed the Bible study beforehand. But in case someone forgot to prepare, the student can still contribute by looking up the verses with the rest of the group and taking part in the discussion. However, the more preparation, the better the discussion will be.

Your goal as the leader is to guide the group through the disciple's journal using the helps and suggestions found in the leader's guide. But most importantly, you want to make sure group members see the answers in their own Bibles. You want them to leave with more than good notes in their journals. You want them to retain God's Word in their hearts. Feel free to add your own insights, illustrations, and practical suggestions to give a personal touch. Encourage each person to take part in the discussion, sharing observations and insights. The way to do this is by simply asking the questions found in the disciple's journal. In this way, you are opening up the discussion to everyone.

At times, one or two eager students may tend to dominate a discussion. Since that can be intimidating to others in the group, direct some of your questions to particular individuals. Say something like, "David, what is this verse teaching us?" Also let each person read Scripture aloud. This is an easy way to draw people into the discussion. By doing this, you are making sure there are no "back row" Bible study members.

C. Reflect and Respond (Application, 5-10 minutes)

The goal of all Bible study is life change. Period. You want to produce more than just smarter Bible students. You want God to use this study to impact what they believe, how they think, and the way they live. And application is the key to this. After discovering what a passage says and after digging into it to find out what it means, you are ready to take what you have learned and make it real in your life. Here you want to brainstorm together on some concrete, practical ways to live out your faith. This is how you go from head knowledge to heart knowledge. You want to walk away knowing how your study changes your life. Sometimes the application will affect what they believe. Other times it will affect how they think. And many times, there will be something they need to do. A simple question to ask at the end of each study is, "How does this study change me?"

3 Sharing and Prayer (15-20 minutes)

Use this time to give each person the opportunity to relate prayer requests, praise God for answered prayer, and share personal concerns with the group. Begin by letting the group come up with at least one application out of your study you can pray for. Then take personal requests. Remember, if it is important to them, it is important to God.

But don't spend all of your time talking about prayer. Spend time actually praying together. Have open prayer, where anyone who feels led can pray out loud. Be creative with your prayer time. You could assign specific requests to certain students, let each person pray for the friend on the right or left, or focus on a particular topic, such as praise, thanksgiving, confession, etc. Be sure to use the prayer page at the end of each week so they can write down their requests and keep a record of God's faithfulness in answering those requests.

Finally, have a definite ending time each week and make sure you end on time. Respect your group members' schedules and don't forget to thank them for coming. If they want to hang around afterwards, that is fine. But be sure they know when the group time will officially be over.

The Disciple's Journal

It is recommended that you work your way through the appropriate session in the disciple's journal as if you were one of the regular group members. This will help you get a feel for what group members will have learned before you supplement their study with information from the leader's guide.

To begin with, you will find that there is usually an intriguing activity or story to spark people's interest in completing the Bible study. Group members can have fun with it while making some exciting discoveries about their relationship with God.

Some, but not all, of the Scripture verses are printed in the journal. We try to print the Scripture whenever there is a Scripture-marking activity—underlining, circling words, etc. However, we strongly encourage people to use their own Bibles as they work through these studies. We used the New International Version and you should too, if possible. But don't worry, use whatever translation you are most comfortable with.

There is space in the journal to write down responses to the questions. If more room is needed, write additional thoughts in some kind of notebook that will be easy to tote with you to the group Bible study. Make sure your notations are complete enough to make sense to you during the small group Bible study time. You may want to write down key words to spark your memory or you may need to write out complete thoughts—whichever works best for you.

There is also room to express oneself on the "Pray About It" page. Write out personal conversations with God. Talk to Him about, well, anything. Keep track of your requests and God's answers.

Encourage group members to always try to complete the entire week's study before the small group meeting, so that they can get the most out of other people's comments. This way, they won't miss out by trying to catch up on reading during the small group time.

WEEK 1 Fanatical Followers!

What Is a Disciple?

Overview

• Introduce group members to the overall concept of discipleship.

• Challenge group members to examine their own hearts and make a commitment to follow Christ fully.

Scripture: Matthew 4:18-22; 9:9 and selected passages about following Jesus

1 Getting Started

Feel free to prepare a few munchies ahead of time to kick off your study time in a positive way. Food will help group members to relax, and give everyone a little extra time to get to know each other better before beginning the study. If your group is meeting for the first time, encourage mingling too.

Housekeeping

Hand out copies of the disciple's journal *No Turning Back.* Let people flip through the journal. As they do, explain some of its different sections, especially the "Pray About It" section at the end of each week. Encourage group members to mark up their journals as they go through the studies. They may want to underline or highlight words, circle key phrases, or jot down notes in the margin.

Icebreaking

Hand out slips of paper and ask group members to write down the names of superheroes they liked as children. Collect the papers and put them in a hat, basket, or bowl. Have group members pair up. Choose one person from each pair to pick a name and try to get his or her partner to guess the identity of the superhero. The person can give clues any way he or she chooses—without saying the superhero's name in any form. For example, if the superhero is Batman, the person could say, "Robin's sidekick." Or for the more creative clue giver: "The wooden stick used in baseball and a male person." Or the even more creative clue giver could act out the clues.

When all the superheroes have been identified, let group members claim their own superheroes and explain why they admired them.

Opening

If someone in the group plays an instrument, ask if he or she would be willing to lead singing each week. You don't have to sing at all, but occasionally we'll suggest songs that go along with the theme.

Here's a prayer you may want to use or adapt as you begin this study.

Lord, thank You for making it possible for us to become children of God. As we discover what it means to be Your disciples, make us aware of the things we need to change in order to follow You 100 percent. In Jesus' name. Amen.

2 Bible Study

Focus

Ask group members to turn to page 11 in the journal and check their reactions to the multiple-choice statements in Section I, "Follow Me."

Talk about the different reactions group members checked off. Feel free to follow up with additional questions such as: **What pictures come to mind when you hear the word "disciple"? Do you know anyone today who is a disciple? What do you think makes him or her a disciple?**

Point out that a disciple in Jesus' day literally followed his master or teacher wherever he would go, step for step! A disciple would give up personal plans and agendas in order to follow the master. A disciple would also imitate the life of the teacher.

 Give group members enough time to read Matthew 9:9 and 4:18-22 in their Bibles and answer the first three questions in Section I.

After talking about the answers, ask: **Why do you think no one politely declined Jesus' invitation?**

If some people want to know why the verses don't mention any female followers of Christ, refer them to John 4—the story about the woman at the well; Matthew 15:21-28—Jesus marveled at the Canaanite woman's faith; and Luke 24:1-9—the women who followed Jesus were the first to hear that Jesus had risen from the dead.

Leader's Tip: Whenever a group member volunteers to read a Bible passage aloud or answers a question, thank him or her. Say something encouraging for every Scripture that has been read, every question asked and answered, and for any contribution to the group discussion. As long as your praise is sincere, you cannot praise people enough for their participation.

 ## Dig In

Read this illustration to the group:

Just because you go into a garage doesn't make you a car. Just because you go swimming doesn't make you a fish. Just because you wear a football jersey doesn't make you a football player. And just because someone was called a disciple back in Jesus' day didn't necessarily mean he or she was a Christian. It's the same way today. Many people say they're "Christians,"

but they have no concept of what it means to be authentic followers of Jesus Christ.

Depending on the person or situation, it may have merely meant that the person was a follower. You might want to remind group members of this difference at various points during this discussion.

Ask someone to read the introduction to Section II, "Three Types of Disciples" (page 13 in the journal). Discuss each kind of disciple one at a time.

 What does it mean to be a "casual" disciple? To answer that, look up John 6:2, 26.

> 1. Why was this huge crowd following Jesus? Why do you think the crowd could be described as casual disciples?

Here are *some* possible reasons why the crowd followed Jesus. Share these only if group members are having difficulty coming up with their own answers. The people were only interested in what Jesus did for them, and totally missed the significance of the miracle of the loaves and fishes. These people followed Jesus just to be entertained by Him and to see what He could do for them.

As group members talk about why the crowd could be described as casual disciples, you might want to briefly tell about a time when you, or someone you knew, fit the description of a casual disciple.

Imagine you're looking at new stereo equipment or a car or some other expensive item. The salesperson walks up and asks if you need help. What do you usually say? "No thanks, just looking." But what's the positive side to just looking at a car, or just looking at the claims of Christ?

The point is that God wants people to seek Him and be curious. A lot of people's relationships with Jesus began when they were just looking for peace, for contentment, for forgiveness.

The second kind of disciple is the convinced disciple. Sounds pretty good, doesn't it? Check out the description on page 13 in your journals.

Ask two people to read John 12:4-6 and Luke 22:1-4. If you'd like, make two lists and compare the different aspects of Judas's commitment. For example, Judas appeared to be concerned about the poor and giving money to them. The other disciples believed he was honest enough to be in charge of the money. The real

Judas, however, cared more about the money than the poor. He was dishonest and stole money. Satan eventually controlled Judas.

Talk about question three in this section. Encourage group members to give specific examples of choices Judas made. Say: **Judas probably went wrong because he never made a total commitment to Jesus. The convinced disciple goes a step further than the casual disciple. He or she claims to believe Christ. The person knows who Jesus is, and even believes He died on the cross as payment for sin, but hasn't experienced a changed heart or new life that comes with trusting Jesus.**

One way to look at these two kinds of disciples is like this: The casual disciple is motivated by emotions or feelings, and the convinced disciple is motivated by the intellect.

You might cross-reference briefly the parable of the sower in Mark 4:1-20. Some of the seed springs up quickly and looks good, but doesn't last. Summarize the content of the parable without having group members turn to it in their Bibles.

It's not enough to be convinced of who Jesus is. We must be committed disciples. Read the following illustration, or let someone else in the group read it.

At a wedding, the minister asks the couple if they are really in love. Of course they reply, "Yes." Then the minister asks, "Do you both get that funny feeling in your stomachs whenever your sweetheart is around?" "Oh, yes!" they gush. Then he gets more personal and asks, "Are you convinced in your minds that you two should really be married? Really sure?" They respond, "Why certainly. We have no doubt in our minds that we are made for each other."

So, is this couple married yet?

No. But why not? They have felt it emotionally. They have believed it intellectually. So what is left for them to do? The answer is that they both have to say, "I do." In other words, the couple has to commit their wills to each other before the marriage ceremony is complete. When they commit all that they are to one another, then they become husband and wife.

How do you think this illustrates a committed disciple of Christ? Brainstorm other ways to illustrate an authentic commitment to Christ.

Have group members read Matthew 4:18-22 again and answer question four in Section II (page 14 in the journal).

Ask people how they summarized the disciples' commitment to Jesus. For example, the disciples left everything to follow Jesus, and this kind of commitment involved their intellect, emotions, and will.

Reflect and Respond

This is a good time right at the beginning of this series to challenge each of your group members to examine his or her relationship and faith in Jesus Christ. So far your questions have primarily related to observation and interpretation of the selected Scriptures. Now the focus changes to application and transformation.

Say: **Take a few minutes to answer questions five, six, and seven in Section II of the journal.**

5. Describe how you think "casual" disciples would act today.

6. How would you describe a "convinced" disciple?

7. What are some ways a "committed" disciple would live out his or her commitment today?

For example, a convinced disciple might be a member of a so-called right church, carry a Bible, have Christian parents, go to a Christian school, know all the Christian lingo, have Christian friends, belong to a Christian club, memorize verses, serve in the church, and never really know the Lord! A casual disciple would approach Christ with a "what's in it for me" attitude.

Ask: **What's the hardest thing about following Jesus today?**

After you've talked about the descriptions and what makes it hard to follow Jesus, ask group members to take a look on page 15 of their journals at the categories that describe the kind of disciples they would be most likely to be.

Explain: **For each category, check off the items that best describe your relationship with Jesus right now. No one will see what you check off, so be completely honest.**

Give group members time to privately mark the appropriate categories. As you notice people who have finished, tell them to start answering the questions in Section IV, "Personal Invitation" (page 16 in the journal).

When everyone has finished answering the questions in Section IV, focus the discussion on questions three and four. Group members probably circled these phrases in Matthew 11:28-30: "come to me," "take my yoke upon you," and "learn from me."

Get several people to share how they rewrote these phrases in their definitions of a disciple.

Say: **Don't answer this next question aloud, but give some serious thought to your answer. Would you describe yourself as a disciple?**

If you feel that you need to explain the basics of the Gospel, and give people an opportunity to trust in Christ, use the information titled, "How to Get Yourself Committed" to explain salvation. It is at the back of the disciple's journal in the "Extra Stuff" section on page 137.

Ask: **What's the hardest thing about making a commitment to Christ?**

If most group members have already trusted Christ for salvation, challenge each of them to renew his or her commitment to Christ as you begin this small group discipleship study.

3 Sharing and Prayer

Encourage group members to not only bring their requests to God but to thank Him for some of the good things that are happening in their lives. Invite them to bring up any prayer request, no matter what the subject—school, grades, job, family, relationships, money, or anything else that is on their hearts.

Make sure that everyone in the group keeps a record of the requests (and answers) in the section at the back of the journal. That way you can have a record of God's faithfulness to you and your group members. Another option is to ask a few volunteers to keep track of the group's requests.

Spend some time in "popcorn prayer," letting anyone who wants to "pop" in and pray. Tell people they don't need to feel pressured to pray out loud, but whoever wants to can.

Encourage people to complete Week Two in time for your next meeting.

WEEK 2 Up Close and Personal

Being with Jesus

Overview

• Let group members take a closer look at Jesus' relationship with His disciples.

• Use Jesus' relationship with His disciples to show that being close to Christ is the result of spending time with Him.

Scripture: Selected passages from the Gospels; Ephesians 1:4

1 Getting Started

Housekeeping

Welcome any new people to the group and give them copies of the disciple's journal. If you feel it's necessary, have group members introduce themselves; then make any necessary announcements. If treats are part of your group time, you can either enjoy them now or after the meeting. It's up to you.

Icebreaking

The point of this activity is to illustrate that the people you are close to and know the best are usually the people with whom you spend the most meaningful time. Go around the group, and ask each person to finish this sentence.

• **Besides my parents, the person who knows more about me than anyone else is . . .**

Follow up this last sentence by asking each person why this person knows so much about him or her. Next, have each person imagine that he or she is stranded on a desert island, and . . .

• Besides the Bible, what two books would you want to have with you and why?

• Okay, so you're not exactly all alone. Who else would you want to be there with you (and not some babe or hunk of the opposite sex!)?

• What do you suppose you would know about this person after a year?

Opening

Sing a simple praise song such as "With Our Hearts" (Don Harris, © 1991 Integrity Music, Inc.) to set the tone for this meeting. Either you or someone else open in prayer. Here's a prayer you might want to use or adapt.

Jesus, it's amazing to realize that You have called us Your friends. And even though all things were created for You and by You, and even though You hold all of creation together, You want to be with us. Thank You for choosing us. Increase our desire to be with You. In Your name we pray. Amen.

2 Bible Study

Focus

Let's assume that group members have finished their journals for this week and are dying to talk about it. First call on someone to read the introduction to Section I, "The Time Factor," and then discuss the open-ended sentence and question that follow.

Think of a close friend you have. If you and your friend were reminiscing, how would you finish this sentence?

Remember the time we . . .

What kinds of things seem to bind you together as friends?

The time factor is at work in your relationship with Jesus. Your closeness to Christ is in direct proportion to the amount of meaningful time you spend with Him.

Say something such as this: **In this chapter, we will learn how this was true in the lives of the original twelve disciples, and why it's true for us. We'll also talk about why we should want to spend time with Jesus.**

Dig In

After talking about questions one and two in Section II, "Being with Jesus," add these questions to the ones in the journal. If group members need time to answer the questions, give them a few minutes to do so.

INSIDE INSIGHTS

■ Jesus did have more than twelve followers. According to Luke 10:1, 17, seventy-two people were sent out by Jesus. These people were sent out two-by-two just as the disciples were.

■ The disciples weren't a homogeneous bunch. There was Simon the Zealot, whose name either described his religious passion or was a reference to Simon's membership in a radical political group who violently opposed the Roman rule. Then there was Matthew, a tax collector. In Jesus' day, tax collectors were Jewish people who worked for the hated Roman government collecting taxes on, guess who, the Jews. Tax collectors were lumped together with "sinners," or notoriously evil people.

Why do you think He only chose twelve? Why not more?

Why do you think Jesus primarily wanted the disciples to be with Him? What does this imply?

If you'd like, point out other people in Scripture whom God chose to use. Say: **God can take the most unlikely candidates and make them great for Him. Who are some people in the Bible you can think of that were "unlikely candidates" whom God used in a great way?**

As a group, read John 17:24 and discuss question three in Section II.

3. What do you think is the big idea in this verse?

To add to the group's understanding of this verse, read (or ask someone else to read) Ephesians 1:4. Ask group members to react to this verse. **What does this tell you about God's purpose in creating people?**

If appropriate, read this illustration.

A young boy went fishing one day with his father. They woke up early in the morning and got all their fishing gear together and started out for the lake. When they arrived, the two of them got their fishing poles ready and began to fish. Not much was said, but the boy thought it was one of the greatest days of his life—just being with his dad.

As the young boy grew into adulthood, he would occasionally tell his friends about the day he went fishing with his dad. After hearing the story many times, a family friend remembered that the boy's father (who was now dead) had kept a journal during those years. The friends did some digging and discovered the journal. Turning to the date of the fishing trip, he only found one sentence: "Went fishing today with my son—a day wasted."

The father totally missed out on what became one of the most important days in his son's life. The son, on the other hand, was content just to be with his dad, and thought it was a wonderful day.

Jesus chose you so that you might be with Him. He's pleased when you simply spend time with Him.

The types of things Jesus did with His disciples tells us what kind of relationship He had with them.

 You might want to give each group member one or two of the Scripture passages to look up and read aloud for question four in Section II. Here are some possible activities: they traveled together; ate together; discussed things; visited people; worked (served) together; and went off by themselves (sort of like a retreat).

Ask: **What do you discover about Jesus' relationship with His disciples from looking at these activities?**

The point you want to make is that Jesus spent time with His disciples doing everyday, ordinary activities. He did this in part so they could develop a relationship with Him, and get to know Him in a personal way.

Say: **What was their relationship like when the disciples were experiencing the ups and downs of life? Could Jesus identify with them in those times too?**

Talk about the matches people made for question five. Make sure people give reasons for their matches. You might consider asking group members which emotion they can most easily identify with.

Once you've come up with a group consensus, talk about question six in the journal. Emphasize the truth that Jesus identifies with His followers today just as He did with the original disciples. Ask if anyone in the group would like to tell about a specific time when Jesus helped him or her deal with a tough emotional situation.

Leader's Tip: Some people feel uncomfortable about revealing personal information. As the group leader, you might want to be the first to talk about vulnerable issues. By doing so, you set the tone for the kinds of things people may want to share.

Reflect and Respond

Say something such as this: **We've talked about why Jesus wants to spend time with you, but why should you spend time with Jesus?**

Spend a few minutes talking about Section III, "Long-term Benefits."

The three benefits people probably discovered are courage—Acts 4:13; knowledge of the Father—John 14:7-9; and peace—John 14:27. These benefits are obviously just the tip of the iceberg. You could add these questions to your discussion.

• **How do you think spending time with Christ will give you courage? Courage for what?**

• **In what way do you think you will get to know the Father by being with Jesus?**

• **Describe the kind of peace Jesus gives. How is it different from the way most people define peace?**

If your group is comfortable and open with each other, talk about the different patterns students saw in their answers as well as their sentence completions for Section IV, "At Home with Jesus."

Take a moment for group members to respond to questions three and four in Section IV. Don't pressure anyone to reply, and if some people need to finish these questions, let them do so privately.

Say: **You should spend time with Christ because of your relationship with Him (He wants to be with you) and you should also spend time with Christ to strengthen your relationship with Him (which benefits you).**

An excellent way to conclude this meeting would be to read aloud all or portions of Robert Boyd Munger's booklet *My Heart—Christ's Home* (available at your local Christian bookstore or from InterVarsity Press, P. O. Box 1400, Downers Grove, IL 60515). You might even want to purchase a copy for each group member. This booklet describes in word pictures how spending time with Christ is not only important to the person, but to Him as well.

▌3▐ Sharing and Prayer

Close your time with prayer. You may want to begin by asking group members to share ways they could make Christ feel more at home in their lives. Let group members know that they are free to not say anything. First, have group prayer for the different things students shared. When you've finished, talk about other requests and pray for them.

Make sure that everyone in the group keeps a record of the requests at the back of the journal. That way you can have a record of God's faithfulness to you and your group members. Encourage group members to read the section, "Putting Some Locomotion in Your Devotions" for practical ways to spend time with Jesus. Remind group members to complete Week Three in the disciple's journal.

Leader's Tip: *If you're meeting in the same place each week, you might consider moving the group time to a different location to emphasize the truth that relationships can be built at a pizza parlor, by a lake, or in a field. Be creative and have fun!*

WEEK 3 Sitting at the Master's Feet

Learning from Jesus

Overview

• Show group members both the importance and the benefits the Bible can have in their lives.

• Enable group members to understand and apply God's Word for themselves.

Scripture: Selected Scripture passages

1 Getting Started

Housekeeping

Bring some extra Bibles in case not everyone brought one to the meeting. Ask people questions about their journals, like when they're doing it and how long it's taking. Make any necessary announcements.

Icebreaking

Ask: **What's the best letter you've ever received? Who was it from? What made the letter so great?**

Next, read the following letter; then ask people to give their interpretations of what the letter writer was trying to say.

Dear Robin,

Hey, what's up? I've been thinking about what happened the other night, and I really feel badly about it. I know that you probably think I don't respect you now, but I want you to know that I do. Sometimes I don't think before I act. I should not have tried to pressure you into doing something you didn't want to do. I hope you don't misinterpret my feelings for you because of this. I really do care about you and "love" you. (I hope you know what I mean by that word!) I think it would be a shame to end our relationship over this one misunderstanding. I need you to forgive me for the way I acted. I still believe in what I said, but maybe my timing was a little off. I could say a lot more and try to explain things better, but there are too many people around.

Anyway, I hope we can patch things up and still be friends. Write or call me soon and let me know how you feel.

Chris

To get things started, ask your group:

- **Who do you think wrote this letter (a girl or a guy)?**
- **When was this letter written?**
- **What is the relationship between these two people?**
- **What was the purpose of the letter?**
- **Why do think this letter was written?**

Some people might think the letter was written by a guy (Chris) who feels bad about pressuring his girlfriend (Robin) into going a little too far on a recent date. While apologizing, he also affirms his "love" for her. But, he is not sorry for what he said. Finally, with time running out, he ends rather abruptly.

When group members have finished interpreting the letter, let them in on the secret: The letter was written by the captain of the football team to his favorite wide receiver!

Explain the background of the letter. Chris had met Robin the first day of practice and the two of them really hit it off. Robin had just moved from another town, where he was a star wide receiver. He and Chris were a great scoring threat on the field. Over the course of the season, they became good friends.

There was only one problem: Chris was a Christian and Robin was a "partyer." Last Friday, Chris finally convinced Robin to go to a Christian concert. They had a great time. After taking their dates home, Chris began to use some of the words to a song they heard at the concert to tell Robin about Christ. Robin really wasn't interested, but Chris kept on talking until Robin finally told him to shut up. Chris got mad and began preaching at him, telling Robin how hot hell was going to be for those who rejected Jesus. Robin got into his car and peeled out, shouting obscenities at Chris as he drove off.

This letter is Chris's attempt to mend the relationship without backing down on what he said about Robin's need for Christ. Because they're both guys, that would explain Chris's comment about using the word "love." The reason Chris cut his letter short is because he was in the locker room when he wrote it and the guys were starting to come in to get dressed for practice.

Say something like this: **This letter illustrates how easy it is to misinterpret and read meanings into words and phrases when we don't know the background or context of the letter.**

This is dangerous when it comes to notes and letters, but it's even more deadly when it comes to understanding and interpreting the Bible. The way we interpret Scripture affects our understanding of who God is and how we are to live as Christians.

Opening

If most of your group members have grown up in the church and are an uninhibited bunch, sing an old childhood favorite, "The B-I-B-L-E." Don't forget the actions! Or you could sing a quieter song like "Thy Word," by Amy Grant. In your opening prayer, thank God for His living Word and ask Him to give all of you a deeper understanding of His truths.

☐ Bible Study

Focus

People can be intimidated when it comes to the Bible. Ask group members for reasons why people don't read the Bible. Keep track of them, and have the group vote on the top five reasons why people don't read the Bible.

Have group members turn to chapter three, "Sitting at the Master's Feet," (page 27 in the journal). As a group, talk about which phrases members circled on the graph to indicate how much or how little they understand the Bible, and why they circled it.

Point out the three questions that this meeting addresses:

"Why is the Bible so important?" "What can the Bible do for me?" and "How can I understand my Bible?"

You might want to ask group members what questions they have about the Bible, and add these questions to the ones in the journal.

Leader's Tip: When you ask people to share questions they have about the Bible or Christianity in general, it's okay to admit that you don't know the answers. But let people know you'll make an effort to find the answers in the next couple of weeks.

Believe it or not, much of the Bible isn't that difficult to understand, but we need to know some basic principles of how to figure out what it means. But first, let's establish the importance of God's Word.

Dig In

Read Luke 10:38-40 to the group, and then ask members how they answered the first two questions in Section II, "Why Is the Bible So Important?" (page 28 in the journal).

 1. Describe how each woman reacted to Jesus' visit.

2. What was the major difference in their responses?

Some things group members may have discovered about the two sisters were that Mary didn't bother to play the perfect host. Meanwhile, Luke 10:40 says that Martha was distracted by the preparations that had to be made. She may have wanted everything to be perfect for Jesus' visit.

One major difference in their responses was that Martha was distracted by the stuff that needed to get done, but Mary was focused on Jesus.

 As a group talk about questions three and four in Section II. Martha's reaction is pretty typical of the way siblings interact, especially when one thinks the other is getting out of work.

Before looking at Jesus' response to Martha in Luke 10:41, 42, ask: **Do you think Martha was wrong for her reaction to the visit? Why or why not?**

 Ask someone to read Luke 10:41, 42 (the verses are printed in the journal) and discuss questions five and six.

As group members talk about Jesus' response, get them to think about Jesus' tone of voice. How did He talk to Martha? Emphasize the importance Jesus placed on listening and learning from Him. Ask: **Why should this be a priority for each Christian?**

Because the Bible comes from God, it has the power to transform us.

 Ask someone to read II Timothy 3:14-17, and then go over the definitions group members came up with for question one in Section III, "What Can the Bible Do for Me?"

Ask: **What are the benefits of knowing the Bible?**

As members wrote their definitions, they probably came across words that sounded important and spiritual, but had no relevance or meaning for them. Here's an explanation of some key words in that passage.

• *Able to make you wise for salvation.* Scriptures clearly present Christ Jesus as the one who died on the cross in our place to pay the penalty for our sin.

• *God-breathed.* This is the basis for the word "inspired." God is the ultimate source of the content of Scripture. God's active involvement in Scripture was so powerful that what's written is the authoritative word of God. The human authors, however, weren't just recorders; they were also active, but what they said came from God.

• *Teaching.* The Bible gives instructions on godly living, who God is, the truth about humanity, and the difference between right and wrong (II Peter 1:2-4).

• *Rebuking.* That doesn't sound like fun. Basically it means the Bible tells you when you've done wrong. It lets you know when you've gotten off track, when you've stepped out of bounds and sinned, and what is not right in your life.

• *Correcting.* What good would it do to know what you've done wrong if you didn't know how to make it right? That is what correcting means. The Bible tells us how to "get right" again—in fellowship with our heavenly Father.

• *Training in righteousness.* Righteousness means holy living. The Bible shows us how to be more like Christ through living as God wants us to.

• *Thoroughly equipped for every good work.* This refers to the good things we do for Christ. The Bible says that God planned for His people to do good works (see Ephesians 2:10). This doesn't mean that we do good works in order to get to heaven or earn God's love. The Bible shows us how to serve Him.

Discuss any definitions group members find hard to understand or accept.

Sum up this passage by something such as this: **In other words, as you read the Bible, you find out how you are suppose to live (teaching). But you sometimes stumble and mess up. That's when the Holy Spirit shows you where you went wrong (rebuking) and how you can get on track again (correcting). Then as you continue in the Word, you discover how to be more consistently Christlike (training in righteousness) and how to serve Him (thoroughly equipped in every good work).**

 Go ahead and ask group members to read the metaphors of God's Word they created for question two of this section. You might want to read Psalm 19:7-11 to get things started. For example, the Bible is like a survival manual because it gives instructions on how to make it in life. Or, the Bible is like glue because it keeps us close to God.

Reflect and Respond

The point you want to communicate is that group members don't have to be afraid of studying and understanding the Bible. Get group members to talk about whether they're Passengers or Adventurers when it comes to Bible reading.

Brainstorm together for ideas to help people understand the Bible better. This would be a good time for the Adventurers to share their "traveling" tips. Here are some suggestions we came up with:

• Get an easy-to-read Bible. You can buy a student Bible, a children's Bible, or even a businessperson's Bible, to name a few.

• Use pen and paper. As you read, write down what you learn in a notebook. Make notes in your Bible—underline, circle, highlight, and jot down special notes or thoughts in the margin.

• Take your time.

• Expect God to speak to you. When you read and study the Bible, there's more going on than just the act of reading and studying. You see, God's Word teaches you and changes you in the process. Approach Bible reading with an open heart and mind. Ask God to speak to you through His Word. Pray for insight into the passage you're reading. Remember, you're not just reading pages, you're spending time with a Person.

Say: **The three questions listed on page 31 in the journal are designed to help you discover God's truth in a particular passage.**

Review the "Look, Learn, Live" section in the journal. Make sure everyone understands the kinds of questions asked in each step. Discuss this idea further, with the example on page 31 of the journal.

The Bible was not only given to inform, but also to transform. It's been said, "Dusty Bibles lead to dirty lives." What's that supposed to mean?

If group members have already completed the mini-Bible study in questions three and four, discuss the different things they found in the passages. If it was a bad week for people and their journals were neglected, choose a few of the passages to look up and discuss.

Mention to your group that it's important not to reverse the order of these three steps as they read and study their Bible. In other words, don't try to apply a passage without first knowing what it means. That's how people end up misinterpreting Scripture.

Encourage group members to begin marking in their Bibles. This disciple's journal could do double-duty as a Bible study notebook. Let them know that what they put into Bible study is what they will take from it. Reassure them that as they take their time, God will speak to them through His Word. Remind them that they are spending time with Jesus, sitting at the Master's feet. This is a good way to approach the Bible.

Here is an option for concluding this meeting.

Choose one or more of these "quips and quotes" about the Bible. Write them on index cards—one card for each group member—to use as a bookmark.

- It is good to mark your Bible, but it is better to let your Bible mark you.
- The best way for Christians to grow is to eat the Bread of Life.
- To master the Bible, the Bible must master you.
- Sin will keep you from this Book, and this Book will keep you from sin.
- The Bible is not only the world's best-seller—it is man's best buy.
- Trying to do away with the truth of the Bible is like trying to mop the ocean dry with a sponge.
- The best thing to do with the Bible is to know it in your head, stow it in your heart, sow it in your world, and show it in your life.
- A well-read Bible is the sign of a well-fed soul.

3 Sharing and Prayer

Spend the rest of the time talking about prayer concerns and praying for each other. Group members may want to use the comparisons they wrote about the Bible as praises to God for His living, life-changing Word. Also record any answered prayer from previous weeks.

WEEK 4 Is Anybody Up There?

Praying Like Jesus

Overview

- Break down misunderstandings people have about prayer.
- Teach group members how to pray based on scriptural principles.
- Show what prayer is and what it isn't.

Scripture: Selected Scripture passages on prayer; Matthew 6:9-13

1 Getting Started

Housekeeping

Take care of any announcements, especially ones about future meeting times and places. This might be a good time to talk about what the group would like to study next.

Ask group members what they think of the group so far. Ask questions such as, "What do you like about our small group?" "What would you change?" "Do you feel the group is meeting a real need in your life?" "If so, in what way?"

Jot down any suggested changes members would like to make. Try to implement some of their changes in the coming weeks.

Icebreaking

As a take-off of the car game "I'm going on a trip, and I'm packing . . .", play "I went to the laundromat to wash. . . ." Go around the group, with the first person naming something to wash with the letter A. The next person has to repeat what the person before said plus come up with something for the letter B, and so on through the entire alphabet. Be as creative as possible. For example, A is for an accordion-pleated skirt; B is for bright blue boxer shorts; C is for a chiffon chemise, etc.

When you've made it through the alphabet, say: **Some people think prayer is like bringing a laundry list to God. How did you pray as a child?**

Opening

Instead of saying a prayer, sing a song as a group prayer. For example, sing the song "Create in Me" (Mary Rice Hopkins, © 1984 by Big Steps U Music).

2 Bible Study

Focus

Prayer is one of those mystical things in the Christian life that sometimes can be sort of scary to relatively young Christians. This meeting will try to demystify the misconceptions people have about prayer.

To gauge group members' feelings about prayer, talk about the prayer habits they identified in response to the opening statement in Section I, "Prayer Habits and Phobias" (page 37 in the journal). Then get people to describe their prayer phobias. For example, "prayalysis" is the fear of freezing when praying aloud, or "snoozeophobia" is the fear of falling asleep during prayer.

Ask: **Which is harder for you—personal prayer or group prayer? Why?**

Most people don't understand the real meaning and purpose of prayer. Suppose you stood outside on a street corner tomorrow afternoon and asked people what prayer is. What kind of responses do you think you would get?

Give each group member an opportunity to answer. Mention that in Jesus' day, things were no different. Most people back then really didn't understand prayer. This was due to the religious leaders' misuse and perversion of prayer (more about that later).

Fortunately, we don't have to depend on opinions to tell us about prayer. We have the Lord's teachings about prayer's real meaning.

  Dig In

 Come up with a group definition of prayer based on what people put down for question one in Section II, "What Exactly Is Prayer?" (page 38 in the journal). The bottom line is that what's going on here is a conversation between Moses and God. They were friends, and friends talk to each other.

INSIDE INSIGHTS

■ When it came to teaching His disciples how not to pray, Jesus pointed to the Pharisees as the number one bad example. In fact, in the New Testament the word "hypocrite" is only used in the four Gospels and only used by Jesus to describe the Pharisees.

■ The word "cast" that's used in I Peter 5:7 is an athletic term that was used in the ancient Olympics when a shot-putter would cast the heavy ball off his shoulders.

■ In the four Gospels, Jesus is the only one who ever addressed God as Father. In His first recorded spoken words in Luke 2:49, Jesus called God His Father. Even at age twelve, Jesus was already aware of His unique relationship with God the Father.

Take a minute to read aloud Psalms 63:6-8 and 69:1-3, and then talk about questions two and three.

 2. What impresses you about the way David, the writer of these psalms, prayed?

3. What else could you add to your definition of prayer?

Point out that David not only prayed when He was up spiritually, but also when He hit bottom. Add anything to the group definition of prayer.

Say: **Some people think that praying in the morning is more spiritual than** praying the last thing at night or kneeling is more spiritual than sitting in a chair. What did you say for question four in the journal?

The point of seeing the different ways people pray is to realize that prayer can take all sorts of forms without one being more spiritual than another. But it's a different story when it comes to a person's attitude regarding prayer.

God does more than hear words—He reads hearts. When it comes to prayer, it's not how you position your body, but how you position your heart.

If you'd like, read the following illustration.

Imagine you had a date Friday night with the most beautiful girl or handsomest guy on campus. Let's make believe this person is a strong, committed Christian. Your cologne or perfume is strategically applied for maximum effect. And to top things off, you're having a good hair day. The time is set; the restaurant table reserved.

• Would you be looking forward to going out or would you be dreading it? (All right, you'd be a bit nervous.)

• Would you get ready early or wait until the last minute?

• Would you be excited about going, or would you rather stay home and watch a documentary on public TV?

• Would the evening be a real pain or a real privilege?

Seriously, if you think about it, prayer is somewhat like that perfect date. Prayer isn't something to dread or avoid or to be nervous about. It is something we get to do and enjoy. Once we begin to see prayer this way, we will want to spend more time talking with our Lord.

According to Jesus, there is a right way to pray and a wrong way to pray.

 Have group members report some of the don'ts of prayer they discovered in Matthew 6:5, 7; Luke 18:10-12; and James 4:3 (Section III, "The Dos and Don'ts of Prayer," page 39 in the journal).

Some of their answers might include the following: don't pray to impress others; don't babble on, using meaningless words; don't pray with a self-righteous attitude; don't pray with a proud heart; don't pray with selfish motives.

As a group, brainstorm ways a person can try to impress others with his or her prayer. Here are some examples.

• Using words which *sound* spiritual, but have little or no meaning to the group. ("Lord, bless and sanctify your servant as he awaits the parousia of Your presence in the knowledge of the holy." Huh?)

• Praying long prayers to appear religious. ("And now, Lord, we turn our attention to the country of Pango Pango. We pray for the missionaries there, beginning with those whose names begin with the letter A.")

• Focusing on people's response ("Wow, that prayer got two 'Amens'!").

Remind your students that when they pray in a group, the primary audience is still the Lord. And when someone else is praying, it helps to pray silently along, agreeing in prayer. This can also help keep your mind from wandering.

Say something such as this: **In contrast to the Pharisees' praying, the Bible clearly shows how to pray.** Read the situation on page 40 in the journal.

"Okay, let's pray," the Bible study leader says. Silence. Then Jason (the "spiritual" one in the group) prays a short prayer. More silence. Meanwhile, Kelly is thinking, *I want to pray, but I don't know what to say other than "Lord, bless so-and-so,"* and *"Be with the missionaries,"* and *"In Jesus' name."* Long, awkward silence. Julia finally prays, remembering to ask God to make Scott's grandmother better. Deadly silence. An unbearable minute longer and the leader closes the prayer time.

Encourage group members to be open in sharing their feelings about group prayer. Ask: **How do you feel during our group's prayer time?**

Change the focus to personal prayer by saying this: **Let's come up with a scenario for someone's personal prayer time.**

Create the scenario as a chain story. Call on someone to begin the story and to keep talking until you say stop. Then the next group member picks up the story, adding different details. You say stop again, and someone else continues the story, building on the plot. The last group member concludes the scenario.

Ask: **Do you think our story is an accurate description of your personal prayer times? Why or why not?**

Leader's Tip: Whenever possible, delegate responsibilities. The more you share the leadership, the more committed group members will feel to the weekly meeting.

Talk about the reasons why group or personal prayer can be uncomfortable or awkward.

Explain that the key is to change our attitude toward prayer. Most students are more likely to be afraid of praying than they are to be self-righteous in prayer. Usually, a student won't pray in a group because he or she is afraid of saying the wrong thing or not sounding spiritual enough. The three passages listed under questionfour (page 40 in the journal) can help break down the barriers of fear about prayer. The purpose here is to help the student see how much God wants him or her to pray about everything, and to realize that Christ has made it possible for us to have access to God the Father.

Here are some additional notes on the verses.

I Peter 5:7. As we go to the Lord in prayer, we can cast our worries, anxieties, fears, and concerns off of our shoulders and onto His. We let Him carry our burdens because He cares so much about us.

Hebrews 4:15, 16. While on earth, Jesus was tempted in the same ways we are tempted today. When we approach God with all of our weaknesses, He won't reject us. He accepts us on the basis of what Christ accomplished on the cross. We can know that God will give us mercy, grace, and help when we need it.

Philippians 4:6, 7. These verses are saying that nothing in life is too insignificant for God. If it matters to you, it matters to God. If it is worth worrying about, it is worth praying about. You should bring both your needs and your wants to the Lord. Verse seven goes on to say that if you do this, God will fill your mind with a peace that is beyond understanding.

 Wrap up this discussion with questions five, six, and seven from the journal (page 41). Have group members give specific reasons for their answers.

Reflect and Respond

Because Jesus wanted prayer to be meaningful, He taught His disciples how to pray. Let's investigate the model prayer He gave and discover how to use it as a foundation for our prayers.

Ask group members to turn to Matthew 6:9-15 in their Bibles, and read it in unison before discussing the questions in Section IV, "Model Prayer." A word of caution: Jesus never meant for the Lord's Prayer to be mindlessly repeated in church or in a locker room before the game. No prayer—written or otherwise—should be repeated mindlessly.

Feel free to add any of these comments to the group discussion.

Adoration. To "hallow" means to esteem, honor, revere, and adore. Interestingly enough, the name of God that we're to honor is Father. To pray "hallowed be your name" is to adore God as Father. Jesus chose the name that states our relationship with God. You can also worship God in prayer through music as well. David did. Many of the psalms were hymns of worship.

Confession. When you confess your sins to God, you are agreeing with Him that you have done wrong in His sight. According to Psalm 66:18, unconfessed sin blocks our prayers and fellowship with God. As you focus on who God is, you will see your own sin more clearly. And as you confess your sin, He will forgive you completely—that's the promise of I John 1:9.

Petition. The word "petition" means to ask God for things, or to present your requests to Him (as you discussed in Philippians 4:6). In this passage, Jesus shows His disciples how to pray for provision ("give us today our daily bread") and protection ("and lead us not into temptation, but deliver us from the evil one"). You should also use this time to pray for others as well (see I Timothy 2:1, 2).

Submission and thanksgiving. When you pray "your kingdom come, your will be done," you're telling God that you're more interested in His plan than your own. You're asking God to accomplish His purposes in the world (and in your own life). It's your way of telling God that you want your life to line up with His will for you. It's a way of putting every area of your life under His control. Also thank God for what He's doing in your life. Thanksgiving acknowledges our dependency on God the Father, the giver of every good and perfect gift.

Ask people what things they checked off that Jesus included in His prayer. Most of them probably caught the one thing Jesus left out—confession.

Use the acrostic for the word "pray" (page 42 in the journal) to reinforce the ideas in the Lord's Prayer. Have people creatively create their own acrostics.

Ask: **How can we know that God will answer our prayers?**

 Ask group members to explain their answers to questions one and two in Section V, "How Can I Know God Will Answer My Prayers?"

James 5:16 teaches us that righteousness, or moral rightness, makes our prayers effective. Ask: **Why do you think moral purity is related to effective prayers?**

The obvious teaching of I John 5:14, 15 is that we can expect God to answer every prayer that is according to His will. But the next logical question is, "How do I know if my request is according to His will?"

Explain: **You can have a pretty good idea by checking out your request with what's in the Word. You will find God's will and desires in the Bible. Ask yourself: *Is it consistent with God's character? Is it in harmony with His Word? How will this glorify Him?***

While God's will for us may not always seem "crystal clear," we should do what Matthew 7:7, 8 says—keep on praying. This way, we can bring our requests to God, confident that He will answer. We also know that when we submit those requests, He will know to do what is best.

3 Sharing and Prayer

Have group members look at the ratings they gave their prayer lives and their response to question one in Section VI, "Personal Prayer," (page 44 in the journal). Spend a few minutes in individual prayer, with each group member talking honestly to God about the changes they want to make. After a few minutes of quiet, you close in prayer this week, without having group prayer.

Challenge group members to spend at least five minutes a day in prayer for the next seven days. Assign the last chapter of this section for next week.

WEEK 5 Lean on Me!

Relying on Jesus

Overview

• Help group members understand that walking with Jesus is a way of life.

• Demonstrate the need for, and the priority of, being filled with the Spirit.

Scripture: Ephesians 1:1-14; 5:18; and selected Scripture passages

1 Getting Started

Housekeeping

With this meeting, you will finish the first unit in this book. Decide as a group if you want a week off or if you want to move right into the second unit. Set a time for your next meeting. If you decide to go ahead with the second unit, tell your group members to prepare for it by reading Chapter Six, which is titled "Cross Training."

Remind group members to keep marking up their journals.

Icebreaking

Ask the group: **Which amusement park ride best describes your spiritual life this past year, and why?**

• **Bumper cars**   • **Water slide**   • **Merry-go-round**

• **Roller coaster**   • **Kiddie land**

Encourage group members to add any more rides to the list you just read.

Explain that this meeting won't guarantee a smooth spiritual ride, but it might help them understand that they can live for Christ consistently.

Opening

A good song to sing at the start of this meeting is "Step by Step" by Rich Mullins (Edward Grant, Inc.) or "Day after Day" by Walt Harrah and John A. Schreiner (Maranatha! Music). Recruit someone to pray, thanking God for what you've learned about being disciples.

2 Bible Study

Focus

Ask group members how they reacted to the story about the farmer from Section I, "Unclaimed Wealth," page 47 in the journal.

Say: **As you begin to grow as a disciple, you realize that you don't have to live the Christian life on your own. In fact, Christ has done it all.**

Dig In

Before looking at Ephesians 1:1-14, ask group members to complete this sentence: **I'd be rich, if I . . .**

Now investigate Ephesians 1:1-14. Compare lists group members came up with for question one of Section II, "It's All Yours" (page 48 in the journal).

For example, God has blessed us with every spiritual blessing in Christ; He chose us before the creation of the world; in love He predestined us and adopted us; in Him we have redemption and forgiveness of sin; He lavished on us all wisdom and understanding; He made His will known to us; He gave us the Holy Spirit as a deposit guaranteeing our inheritance.

There's a lot in these fourteen verses. Check out some of these blessings in detail. When you've finished discussing this passage, ask group members to complete another sentence: **I am rich because Christ . . .**

If Christ has done it all for us, what's our part?

As a way of answering that question, ask someone to read the illustration about walking on the frozen pond in Section III, "You Can Depend on Jesus" (page 49), and answer questions one and two.

Some possible answers students may give for question two are "because He's the one you trust in and depend on," and "He's the basis of your faith."

Say: **Obviously the thickness of the ice is more important than the amount of a person's faith. But how do you know the ice is really six-feet thick? How do you know you can trust Jesus?**

Talk about this question for a few minutes. In contrast to Satan, who has been deceiving people from the beginning, Jesus is all truth. He keeps His word.

Have your group members describe the emotions they checked off for question three and read their paraphrases of Jesus' promises. You might want to read aloud a few of these verses as an encouragement to the group.

Unfortunately, we don't always turn to Jesus to meet all those needs. Ask your group: **Where else do we turn?** Discuss this for a moment.

Emphasize this point: **Christ can be trusted and depended on in everyday situations to help you overcome feeling defeated and hopeless!**

Leader's Tip: *Unless the whole group wants to talk about a certain issue, don't get off on a tangent. Otherwise, you'll risk boredom or even resentment toward the person who monopolizes the discussion.*

I N S I D E

■ The word "blessing" (Ephesians 1:3) refers to the spiritual good brought by the Gospel.

■ When Scripture refers to the "head," it is not merely referring to the seat of the intellect but regards it as the source of life. That's why people covered their heads with the hand or with dust and ashes to mourn the loss of life. So, according to Ephesians 1:10, all things in heaven and on earth will be brought together under one head, Christ, who is the source of life.

Reflect and Respond

To begin Section IV, "How Do I Rely on Jesus?" (page 50 in the journal), read Ephesians 5:18. Ask group members what the two commands are in this verse. (Don't get drunk and be filled with the Spirit.)

Ask students how they compared and contrasted these two commands. Besides making a person look stupid, alcohol influences or controls a person's thoughts and actions. Being drunk can make someone do things he or she wouldn't ordinarily do. It causes a person to act differently.

Just as alcohol influences or controls a person, the Spirit influences and controls the person who is filled with the Spirit. Yet the Spirit doesn't control a person as if he or she were a robot or a remote-control car. Instead, God chooses to work through a person's strengths, gifts, and abilities.

Say: **Being filled with the Spirit also enables Christians, like Peter, to do things they ordinarily wouldn't do. After Jesus was crucified, he went into hiding, afraid of the local authorities. But once he was filled with the Spirit at Pentecost (see Acts 2), he stood up and boldly preached to thousands, and three thousand people trusted Christ.**

To illustrate the results of being controlled by the Spirit, have group members report what they discovered from the verses in question three in Section IV (page 51 of the journal).

3. Read the following verses and explain what happens when the Holy Spirit is in control of your life.

• Galatians 5:22, 23   • Ephesians 5:19, 20   • Colossians 3:16, 17

When a person is filled with the Spirit, there's a godly change in his or her attitude and actions. The Spirit produces godly qualities such as joy and gentleness.

Ask: **What's our role in being filled with the Spirit?**

To answer this question, ask students to look up Romans 12:1 and Galatians 5:16 in their Bibles. Our role is to allow Christ to control us.

Say: **You don't have to say an "official prayer" to be filled, but you do have to make a choice to live by the Spirit. When you allow Christ to fill you, you are not "getting saved" again. You are simply, at that moment, restoring Jesus to the place He rightfully belongs in your life—in control.**

As question four in this section states, have group members summarize in their own words what they think it means to be filled with the Spirit. Some responses you might hear are: Christ having total control of your life; changes in the way you act and think; living a godly life, etc.

Give group members an opportunity to reflect and pray about the situations and relationships they mentioned in the last two questions in this section. Let people add anything to their original responses if they wish to do so.

3 Sharing and Prayer

Go from this time of individual prayer to group prayer. If people want the prayer support of the group for a situation or relationship, encourage them to give specific ways the group can help them and pray for them.

After prayer, this would be a great time to summarize what you've covered in this book before you move on to the next unit, "Following Jesus." Ask group members to flip through their journals. What have they learned? What has been the most helpful?

Here's a short review of the chapters you've just completed.

Chapter One—To be a genuine disciple, we must be more than curious or intellectually convinced. We must be fully committed to Jesus Christ.
Chapter Two—Jesus chose us so we could be with Him. The time we spend with Christ is vital to keeping our relationship with Him close, strong, and exciting.
Chapter Three—Just as His disciples spent time at Jesus' feet listening to God's Word, we can do the same today as we take time to study the Bible.
Chapter Four—We discovered the dos and don'ts of prayer, and learned to do more than "say" a prayer.
Chapter Five—We discovered what it means to be filled with the Spirit.

WEEK 6 Cross Training

Counting the Cost of Following Christ

Overview

- Help group members understand the cost involved in following Jesus.
- Encourage group members to live out their commitments to Jesus.

Scripture: Luke 14:25-35

1 Getting Started

Housekeeping

If new people have joined your group, make sure they get journals. Bring them up to speed with a quick review of the first five chapters. Mention these aspects of discipleship: following Jesus, being with Jesus, learning from Jesus, praying to Jesus, and relying on Jesus. Have current group members share what they gained from the first section in the book.

Icebreaking

Encourage group members to have fun coming up with creative excuses for (choose two or three):

- getting out of a date
- missing a deadline
- standing up a friend
- being out of shape

- arriving late to work
- skipping a dental appointment
- bowing out of a family event

The goal is to top everyone else's excuse. Play a practice round before you begin. Have group members vote on the top excuses in each category; then have those players compete to determine the best excuse-giver in the group.

Opening

Choose a song about following Jesus if your group has been singing each week. Then say: **As we continue to look at what it means to follow Jesus, we're going to discover how this relates to some practical areas such as maintaining a strong commitment to Christ, dealing with Satan and sin, having Christian friendships, following God's will, and serving others.**

Here's a prayer for you to use or adapt for the study. **Jesus, when You called Your disciples to follow You, You meant business. And You still mean business when You invite us to follow You today. Help us to make our commitment to You the main thing in our lives. In Your name. Amen.**

2 Bible Study

Focus

Ask people to turn to page 56 in the journal, and show off the symbols they created for question three in Section II, "More Than Anything." Have them explain the symbols and talk about these close relationships.

Ask: **How would you describe your commitment level to these people?** Let people respond.

In Jesus' day, people who followed Him because they wanted an easy life were in for a big surprise. Why? Because following Jesus wasn't easy then—and it isn't easy now.

Ask for people's thoughts on the strong words Jesus used to describe what a commitment to Him requires.

Have someone read Luke 14:25-35 out loud.

Dig In

Backtrack and talk about question two in Section II of the journal.

2. What do you think Jesus meant when He talked about hating your father, mother, sisters, and brothers?

When Jesus used the word "hate" He was using hyperbole (exaggeration) to make His point. Jesus defined what He meant by hate in Matthew 10:37. We must love Jesus more than we love anyone else—including ourselves. By comparison, our love for anyone else appears as hate.

Have people think of other examples of hyperbole to express the same idea. For example, in monetary terms, your love for Jesus should be worth a million dollars, and your love for anyone else should be worth a penny!

Ask: **How does your love for Jesus compare with your love for the people you listed for question three?**

Leader's Tip: *Part of your role as a group leader is to know when to push the limits and get people to be vulnerable and when to back down. Pray for sensitivity.*

Instruct group members to add a fourth symbol that represents their relationship with Jesus and His importance to their lives to the ones they already drew on page 56 in their journals. Give group members a chance to explain their drawings.

Ask someone to reread Luke 14:26, and focus on question five in Section II.

Depending on your discussion, you might want to point out that a healthy self-love means seeing yourself as God sees you—forgiven (because you are a sinner), made righteous through Christ, and loved by God. An unhealthy self-love is when you live only for yourself.

How does this help you understand what Jesus meant in Luke 14:26?

Jesus is saying your love for Him must far outweigh your love for yourself. In other words, the way you live your life is not ultimately for you, but for Him.

But Jesus went even further in verse 27 and gave a third characteristic of a "cross"-training disciple. Discuss question seven.

 7. According to Luke 14:27, the person who follows Jesus has to "carry his cross." What do you think this phrase means? What do you think the crowd immediately thought of when Jesus said the word "cross"?

If it will help people, read out loud the information about the cross in the Inside Insights section on page 51.

Does this mean that every person who follows Jesus will end up dying for the cause? Why or why not?

Actually, the answer to this question is yes and no. A lot of people have died for their faith, including some of the original disciples. Jesus called for the ultimate commitment here. He challenged people to submit their lives completely to Him, to die to their own lives, and to live for Him each day.

As a group, come up with examples of what it means to carry one's cross today. For example:

• Your material possessions are His material possessions.
• Your car is His car.
• Your time is His time.
• Your mind is submitted to His control.
• Your talents are under His direction.
• Everything you are and have is His. You exist for Jesus. He is your reason for living.

Ask: **How many of you have heard or used the term "count the cost" when**

you're talking about following Jesus? What do you think it means?

Explain to group members that this expression could trace its roots to Luke 14:28, where Jesus described a builder estimating the costs of the project.

Talk about questions two and three in Section III, "Serious Stuff" (page 57 in the journal). Both the builder and the king had to estimate the cost to see what they were up against. The point is that Jesus doesn't want people to make a naive commitment and expect only blessings and good times. He wants people to count the cost and to understand what He expects of them.

Explain that this is not to say that there are no benefits to a relationship with God. Ask group members to describe some benefits and find verses that mention the benefits. A few to get people started if they need help are Matthew 28:19, 20 (Jesus promises His presence); Galatians 5:22 (love, joy, peace, etc.).

What does Jesus expect from His followers?

The answer in Luke 14:33 is pointed: "In the same way, any of you who does not give up everything he has cannot be my disciple."

As a group, brainstorm what it costs a person to follow Christ today. Encourage people to give specific examples of how a sold-out commitment to Jesus affects their relationships, actions, attitudes, career choices, and other areas.

A commitment to Jesus is not something to enter into lightly. Following Christ is the most important thing you will ever do—more important than your school, your friends, your family, future spouse and children, or your career.

In His last illustration, Jesus used ordinary salt. It sounds elementary, but salt's main characteristic is its saltiness. Without the saltiness, it's worthless.

Ask someone to read Matthew 5:13, and then talk about question six in Section III.

According to the context of this passage, a disciple's saltiness is his or her total commitment to Jesus. That's the distinctive mark of an authentic disciple. If our commitment and love for Christ is missing, we've lost our distinctiveness.

Reflect and Respond

Ask: **What do you think is the hardest thing about being totally committed to Jesus?**

The "cost" might be different for each person in the group, but Jesus still wants His followers to give up everything and follow Him. Encourage group members to also explain why it is worthwhile to follow Jesus. Refer them to the "Keep In Mind" section that identifies some of the benefits of following Christ. Let them talk about the benefits they added to that list.

You might want to ask people to recall specific events that made them realize that a sold-out commitment to Jesus is the only way to live. This could be a positive experience for the group as you affirm each other's decision to follow Jesus no matter what happens.

3 Sharing and Prayer

Close in prayer. You might want to begin first in silent prayer, giving group members a chance to pray the prayer they completed in the journal (Section IV, "Cutting or Counting Costs," page 59). Encourage members to express their commitment to Christ during prayer.

Encourage your group members to love and follow Jesus above anyone and anything in the coming week. Then encourage them to grab some refreshments. Also remind them to complete Week Seven for next week's meeting.

WEEK 7 War Zone

Battling Spiritual Enemies

Overview

- Help group members recognize the spiritual battle around them.
- Identify spiritual enemies that a follower of Jesus confronts.
- Understand that God helps His people fight the temptation to sin.

Scripture: Selected passages about temptation and spiritual enemies

1 Getting Started

Housekeeping

If you need to pass out journals to new group members do so. Make any announcements.

Icebreaking

This idea will get the group thinking about the spiritual realm. Have group members imagine they can observe the invisible spiritual realm. Ask what they might see:

- at a hospital as a terminally ill patient dies
- at a party
- in heaven (what would it look like)
- in a classroom during final exams
- in a courtroom during a bitter divorce settlement

If desired, let people make goofy glasses to wear during the activity (or the entire meeting if someone really wants to). Buy some wild-colored pipe cleaners to use for the glasses (you need four pipe cleaners for each pair of glasses).

Opening

You might want to sing "The Battle Belongs to the Lord" by Jamie Owens-Collins (© 1984 Fairhill Music. Adm. by Word, Inc., ARR. UBP.).

Move into the study time by saying something such as this: **Our study is a serious topic, but we don't have to get down or feel helpless about our spiritual enemies because we are in Christ, and Christ is greater than Satan.**

Here's a prayer to use or adapt for the study. **Heavenly Father, the real struggle as we follow You involves spiritual enemies who attack us and tempt us to sin. It's only in Your power and by Your grace that we can take our stand against these enemies. You are greater than our enemies and we can trust You even when the battle becomes intense. In Jesus' name. Amen.**

2 Bible Study

Focus

Suppose that the Internal Revenue Service instituted a tax on sin. How could the tax be structured? Would the tax be higher for repreat offenders and lower for first-time offenders? What do you think is a fair tax on the sins included in the chart in the journal on page 63?

Have people work in pairs on their sin tax proposals. Let them present their ideas to the group and explain their thinking. Come to a consensus about the new tax code. Then ask: **According to this new tax code on sin, how much would you owe for the year?** (Give people time to figure this out. They can keep their findings to themselves.)

What could you do to lower your taxes? After responses, say: **It's important to realize that the temptation to sin isn't sin. Sin is when a person gives in to the temptation. And Satan will make that sin as attractive as possible.**

Leader's Tip: Respect people's privacy. Some people freely talk about struggles and personal issues. Other people find talking about personal issues the struggle. As long as everyone knows that the small group is a safe place to share struggles, there's no need to pressure anyone.

Dig In

Ephesians 6:12 gives us some vital information about the war we're involved in. How did you describe it?

Give group members a chance to show their sketches or to explain their answers for question one in Section II, "Prepare for Battle." For starters, the war is a spiritual, or supernatural, war. Human opponents aren't the real enemy. Check out the Inside Insights section for additional comments about these powerful beings. The war is fought in the spiritual realm, on the battlefield of our hearts and minds.

INSIDE
INSIGHTS

■ It has been speculated that in all of recorded civilization, there has only been a total of thirteen years when a physical war hasn't been going on somewhere in the world.

■ A comment about the rulers, authorities, powers, and spiritual forces of evil in the heavenly realm: These categories of spiritual beings suggest an organized hierarchy. And we're not talking about the kinds of creatures you see in horror films. We're talking beings that are more evil and more diabolic than most of us can imagine. These beings don't have the run of the highest heaven where Christ is seated at the Father's right hand (see Ephesians 1:22) or where believers are seated with Christ (Ephesians 2:6), but they move freely about the rest of creation.

■ Think of the word "conform" in Romans 12:2 as being pressed into a mold, like clay. Whatever the shape of the mold, that's what the clay becomes. The clay allows the mold to shape it.

Now discuss the next question in the journal.

2. Wouldn't it be easier if you could see your enemies and just blow them away? Look up II Corinthians 10:3, 4, and then II Corinthians 6:6-8. What kinds of weapons do you use in this war?

II Corinthians 10:3, 4 teaches us that our weapons are spiritual as well. We don't rely on human resources, but God's power.

Point out the main weapon in II Corinthians 6:6-8—the Holy Spirit. Mention that people tend to want to fight with weapons such as gossip, slander, or abusive speech that would hurt others, which is actually playing into Satan's hands. This passage takes the opposite approach. Fight back with purity, understanding, patience, and kindness, and with weapons of righteousness.

Why do you think these kinds of weapons are effective in fighting against these powerful beings? Encourage group members to give specific examples of how purity or sincere love or another weapon is effective in the spiritual battle. Preferably, they can offer some personal examples.

Say something such as this: **Anyone who has ever played team sports knows that one successful strategy is to know the opposing team well. Know its offense, its defense, its key players, and the team's strong points and weak points. Even though our spiritual opponents aren't the crosstown rivals, we can benefit from learning more about them.**

 The two Scripture passages listed in question one of Section III, "Behind Enemy Lines," reveal a different influence the world has on us. First, how did you define the concept of world in these two passages?

Explain that when the Bible speaks of the "world" in this way, it isn't talking about the created world that God loved and Jesus died for. The world here means the evil system of the world with its ungodly values. It's the sphere that's under Satan's rule and control and is dead-set against God.

Ask: **What are some ways Christians are tempted to accept the world's way of thinking, its standards, and its values?** Talk about the attraction the world has, and why it's hard to fight this enemy.

Next, discuss question four in Section III.

 4. Read II Corinthians 4:4; Ephesians 2:2; and I Peter 5:8. Come up with some facts about Satan to shatter the myths.

Compare the myths about Satan with the truth about him from these three Scriptures. For example, a myth is that Satan doesn't exist. The truth based on

II Corinthians 4:4 is that Satan, the "god of this age," has blinded the minds of people. Or the myth that Satan is a funny little creature with horns and a pitchfork, but the fact based on I Peter 5:8 is that Satan prowls like a roaring lion, looking for victims to devour. Ephesians 2:2 describes Satan as the "ruler of the kingdom of the air." Satan controls the evil beings who operate in the supernatural realm.

Leader's Tip: In a study about spiritual warfare, it's easy to get sidetracked by telling sensational stories about Satanism. As the small group leader, take the initiative to interrupt a story (especially one that doesn't relate to the discussion) to get things back on track.

Why do you think a Christian's sinful nature is listed as a spiritual enemy?

Have someone look up and read Romans 7:18-21. Ask: **How would you describe what's going on in these verses?**

Every Christian experiences this spiritual tug-of-war, with the Holy Spirit at war with the sinful nature pulling in the other direction (Gal. 5:16). And that pull can be awfully tempting at times.

Go over the stages of temptation in James 1:13-15. For example, a person is first dragged away and enticed by his or her own evil desire; that desire becomes sin; and sin ultimately leads to death. It's a simple formula of desire, sin, and death.

It's time for some group thinking about a practical battle plan for fighting the spiritual battle. Ask people to explain some of their ideas from the journal (Section IV, "Choose to Win," question one); then come up with a consensus on the best strategies for battling spiritual enemies. Any strategy is valid as long as group members can back it up with Scripture—either the passages listed in the journal or other ones they know.

Here are examples of strategies based on the six passages in the journal.

• Psalm 119:9-11—Memorize and obey Scripture. That's what Jesus did when Satan tempted Him. He used a weapon that's available to everyone.

• Hebrews 12:1-3, 12-16—Stick it out and know how easily sin can trip you up. It's easy to get messed up by sin, give up, and forget about following Jesus. The writer of Hebrews wanted believers to tough it out and make it to the finish line, because it will be worthwhile. If you're aware of sin, you'll make the effort to live a holy life and encourage other believers to do the same.

• Galatians 6:1, 2—Be accountable to someone and be ready to restore the person who sins. God never intended for His people to fight spiritual battles alone.

• Ephesians 6:18—Pray. This verse is a reminder that the battle is spiritual and needs to be fought in God's strength, depending on God through prayer.

• James 4:7-10—Resist the devil. Choose to submit yourself to God and He'll give you the power to resist Satan.

• II Timothy 2:22—Run. Don't play with fire. There is a time to just get up and go. Remember Joseph? Flirting with temptation, especially sexual temptation is like a child playing with a loaded gun. Sometimes you just need to flee.

Encourage your group to memorize these verses and principles.

 ## Reflect and Respond

Discuss together any questions about sin and temptation that people might have. Or ask the following questions:

What can I do when I blow it and give in to temptation? Confess your sin to God and ask Him to help you stand your ground the next time.

But what if I keep failing in the same area over and over again? Good news: God doesn't hold your sin against you, and He understands your weaknesses. You probably need a friend to encourage you, someone to help you weave biblical principles into your lifestyle. Find someone to be your accountability partner.

But have other believers struggled with sin and temptation? Remember David, Samson, and Joseph? Some of these people gave in; others didn't. The struggle is part of the spiritual battle.

3 Sharing and Prayer

Ask group members to share any answers to prayer over the last week. If your group has been open with each other, members will probably feel free to talk about the different sins they're struggling with. Close in group prayer, praying for each other in the struggle against sin and temptation.

Before group members leave, encourage them to complete Week Eight for your next week's meeting.

WEEK ⟨8⟩ Significant Others

Strengthening Your Christian Friendships

Overview

• To help group members discover the importance of Christian fellowship.

• To provide tools for people to deepen relationships with Christian friends.

Scripture: Acts 2:41-47; Galatians 3:26-28; Ephesians 4:1-6; Hebrews 3:12-14

1 Getting Started

Housekeeping

As a group, look at the meeting times and places you set up weeks ago. Decide if they still work for the group, and make any changes to the schedule. This is also a good time to encourage more people to get involved in leadership. They've had a chance to observe how it's done and might want to try their hand at it too.

Icebreaking

Group members will need blank paper. Ask people for five different categories, such as types of vegetables, kinds of fruits, or animals. Repeat the categories you hear first and have group members write these down. Next, ask for three letters of the alphabet.

Explain: **You have one minute to write down something for each category that begins with each of the letters. Think of unique things, because you'll score one point for each item you have that no one else does. For example, if the category is animal and one of the letters is A, skip the urge to write "alligator"; instead write "addax." It's also okay to leave categories blank.**

After a minute, have group members read their lists, crossing out any duplicate answers. The person with the most unique answers is the winner.

Play a second round of the game with new categories and letters, only this time—group members want to have the same answers as everyone else. For example, if the category is types of trees, put down "maple" instead of "manchineel" for the letter M. Again, read the lists, crossing out any unique answers. The winner is the person who had the most duplicate answers.

Ask: **Which round was harder for you to play and why?**

How do you handle situations where everyone is different from you? What do you do? What do you say?

Have you ever met someone for the first time and felt an instant bond with the person? Talk about some of these instant bonding relationships.

Opening

Go around the group and say positive things about each other. Or in the opening prayer, you and whoever else prays could thank God for each group member.

We're going to talk about why it's important to maintain our friendships with other Christians and the effects they can have.

2 Bible Study

Focus

Take a survey and have group members raise their hands if they wrote similar things in their journals (page 69) for what they wanted out of life.

- Money
- Children
- Success
- House
- Marriage
- Good friends
- Relatively good health
- Good relationship with family

Chances are that most group members probably included marriage or other relationships as one of the main things they want out of life. No surprise. In a survey, 168,000 teenagers were asked to list the ten most important things they wanted in life, and the top answer was a close relationship with someone.

Emphasize the truth that Christianity is all about relationships—first with God and then with people.

 Next, discuss how group members defined the word "fellowship" in question one of Section II, "Common Ground." Some group members may understand what's involved in Christian fellowship. The point here is that we toss around a lot of words in the Christian community without knowing what they really mean, or the words lose their meaning altogether.

Say "agree" or "disagree" if you think Christian fellowship includes

- **parties**
- **belonging to the same church**
- **being part of a Christian organization**
- **eighty Christians in the same room**
- **believing the same things about God.**

Explain: **All those things are fine, but they are not biblical fellowship itself. So let's go directly to the Word and find out what fellowship involves.**

For a change of pace, try this little experiment to illustrate the way the word "fellowship" has been watered down. You'll need a liter of cola and some paper cups. Before your group begins, pour a little cola into the cups. Next, add a lot of water to each cup. Keep the cups out of sight until this point in the meeting, and then hand them out.

Let group members drink the watered down cola; then give them a taste of the "real thing." Explain that the real thing—authentic fellowship—is always better than a watered-down version that many Christians have.

Move into a discussion about the Acts 2 passage in the journal.

Dig In

Call on someone to read Acts 2:41-47, and then ask people to explain what key words and phrases they underlined. Get group members' responses.

Ask: **How would you describe the relationship these early Christians had with each other? How well do you think you would have done in this close, relational setting?**

To help group members understand this passage better, explain some of the information about fellowship from Inside Insights.

The common ground we have in Jesus can be described in other ways as well. How did you summarize the main points of Galatians 3:26-28 and Ephesians 4:1-6 in question three?

■ The word "fellowship" in Acts 2:42 is from the Greek word "koinonia" (pronounced coin-o-NEE-ya). It sounds like a secluded vacation spot in Hawaii, but actually, the word means "to be partners" or "to be joined together." It has the idea of sharing something with someone. In other words, these first Christians had common ground on which to worship and pray and give.

■ Also in this passage there's a distinction between what these first Christians did as a group and what they did in their daily lives—but one affected the other. For example, the breaking of bread in verse 42 seems to indicate the Lord's Supper, and in verse 46 breaking bread in their homes was simply eating a meal—which they did with gladness and generosity.

■ The word "encouragement" is from the Greek word "parakaleo [parr-ah-kah-LEH-oh]," which means "one called alongside to help or comfort." It's from the same word Jesus used when He described the Holy Spirit as a Counselor or helper (see John 14:16).

For example, the Galatians passage states that believers are one in Christ and there are no barring ethnic, social, or sexual distinctions. The Ephesians passage says that Christians are to keep the unity of the Spirit, and reminds believers that they were called to one hope, one Lord, one faith, one baptism, and one God and Father of all.

Ephesians 4:3 clues us in that it takes work to maintain this unity and oneness in Christ.

As a group, brainstorm things that block unity as well as things that promote unity in the body of Christ.

Leader's Tip: *Some discussions beg to go off on a zillion tangents. It's okay to let the discussion wander as long as most of the group wants to talk about the tangential subject—and it's not one person's hobbyhorse or pet peeve.*

 Ask group members to read their revised definitions of fellowship based on the Bible passages you've just looked at (question four in Section II, page 71 in the journal).

For example, fellowship can be defined as sharing our lives based on our common partnership in Christ. In other words, we influence and build up each other as we center our relationships around the Lord.

Okay, now that we've defined fellowship, why you think it is so important for us to have it?

To answer that question, ask someone to read Hebrews 3:12-14; then talk about questions three and four in Section III, "An Encouraging Word."

 3. What do you think the word encouragement means? Does it have a different meaning when you think in terms of "Christian" fellowship? Why or why not?

4. List five realistic ways you can encourage your Christian friends. Also, think of ways people have encouraged you.

Add this information to the discussion of question three. Encouragement involves more than a pat on the back. It might mean a gentle correction of a wrong or an urgent piece of advice. (See II Corinthians 1:3-5; Hebrews 12:5.)

Ask: **How could correction be encouraging?**

Have group members look at Hebrews 3:13—one of the goals of encouraging each other is to prevent us from becoming hardened by sin's deceitfulness. We need to motivate each other to grow in our relationship with Jesus.

What has been one of the most encouraging things anyone has ever done or said to you? Why was it so encouraging?

Reflect and Respond

Look at your answers for questions one, two, and three in Section IV, "The Ins and Outs of Peer Pressure" (page 72 in the journal). **With these in mind, silently respond to these questions.**

Pause after each question to give group members a chance to think of their honest responses.

• **Do you follow your own advice in choosing your friends? Why or why not?**

• **Would your friends confront you if you did something wrong? Would you confront your friends? What does this say about your relationship?**

• **Do your friends motivate you to make wise choices? If so, how?**

• **Do your friends understand your values as a follower of Jesus? Are your closest friends Christians too?**

If you think it's appropriate, talk about the next question from Section V, "The Fellowship Factor" (page 74 in the journal).

Are we a close group? What can we do to become closer? How can we be more dependent on each other and more open? How can we deepen our friendships? How can we show we care for one another?

3 Sharing and Prayer

Let group members discuss people who have influenced their relationships with Jesus. In your prayer time, encourage group members to express thanks to God for these people.

Take time for personal prayer requests and notes of praise. Then pray for each other. Remind group members to complete Week Nine for your next meeting.

WEEK 9 The Great Mystery

Finding God's Will for Your Life

Overview

• To discuss questions and answers group members may have about God's will.

• To understand what God's will includes for God's people.

Scripture: Jeremiah 29:11; Ephesians 1:9-14

1 Getting Started

Housekeeping

This might be a good time for another small group check. Ask people how they feel about the way group time has been spent. Would they like to change anything? What suggestions do people have for making the small group even better than it already is?

If you want to do something different and you have a short announcement to make, turn the announcement into a word puzzle such as a word search, word scramble, or cryptogram. Make enough puzzles for each group member to solve. Hand out the puzzles at the start of the meeting, and whoever solves it first gets to make the announcement.

Icebreaking

Play a version of the ancient TV game show, "To Tell the Truth." Hand out paper and ask group members to write down a funny or not-too embarrassing story that happened to them. People need to put their names on their stories. Collect the stories and choose one to read.

Next, pick three people to play "To Tell the Truth," making sure the story belongs to one of them. Explain to the group that the story actually happened to one of these people, and members may ask questions to help them figure out whose story it is. The person whose story is read has to tell the truth, but not necessarily tell all; and the other two people have to tell convincing lies about the story. Read the story and then let the questioning begin. You might want to limit the number of questions so you can play more than one round. Whoever guesses correctly may play in the next round.

Ask: **How many of you feel like you're playing a guessing game when it comes to discovering God's will? Why do you feel that way?**

Opening

A good song to sing for this meeting is "You Are the Source" by Glenn Kaiser (© 1993 Grrr Music, ARR, UBP.). To open, adapt Colossians 1:9-12 as a prayer for your group. For example:

Heavenly Father, please reveal Your will to us by giving us spiritual wisdom and understanding. Help us to live lives worthy of You. May we please You in every way. We want to obey You, know You better, and be strengthened by Your mighty arm so that we persevere and learn patience. We joyfully give thanks to You for qualifying us to share in the inheritance of Your kingdom. In Jesus' name. Amen.

2 Bible Study

Focus

Begin by reading the following situation to the group:

Thea is a senior, about ready to make her first major decision concerning college. She has just been awarded a full scholarship to the state university. She's excited, but sort of had her heart set on attending a Christian college in another state. Unfortunately, the school has limited scholarship

funds. Her parents also have limited funds, but were glad to hear the scholarship news from the university. Thea has seriously considered going into missions after college, but she also enjoys studying business. Her biggest fear is that she'll miss God's will for her life if she makes the wrong choice.

So what advice would you give her?

Get group members to weigh the pros and cons of Thea's situation as well as address Thea's real fear of missing out on God's will for her life.

Ask: **Could you relate to Thea's fear about God's will? If so, why?**

Ask group members to share some of the questions they wrote down in their journals about God's plans. If one question keeps popping up, write it down and check back with the group at the end of the meeting to see if it has been answered.

A lot of Christians talk about finding God's will, doing God's will, and waiting on God's will, but exactly what are they talking about?

Have someone read the statements in question one, Section II, "Positive Plans," and ask group members to raise their hands when they agree with a statement.

Dig In

Everywhere you look in the world, you discover God's plan for the way creation works. And it's no different with you—God has plans for His people. It's really less of a mystery than we make it out to be.

Ask someone to look up and read Jeremiah 29:11, and then talk about the different reactions to this verse. **From the way God's plans are described, what can you discover about Him?**

Talk about questions three and four in Section II, "Positive Plans."

Do you think of God's will as good, pleasing, and perfect to us? Explain.

Turn that around and let's think of God's will as being good, pleasing, and perfect to Him. What difference does that make?

When you do that, you end up thinking about God's character and what pleases Him. And what pleases Him is our obedience to Him and our godly lifestyles.

How does that change the way you think of God's will for your life?

It's okay if group members have different opinions about God's will. You might want someone to look up and read Psalm 32:8, and then talk about the ways God instructs and teaches His people—particularly, through His Word.

Spend time investigating Ephesians 1:9-14 (question one, Section III, "Direct Route," page 79). Here are some extra comments that help explain the passage. Also, check out the information about this passage in the Inside Insights section.

• In verse 9, Paul, the author, used the word "mystery" to refer to something that was formerly hidden but is now revealed by God.

• The mystery that God has revealed is His plan to bring everything in heaven and on earth under Christ's headship.

• Christ is the center of God's plan. In Him, we were chosen by God to be His children (Ephesians 1:5). And in Him, God's plans will be accomplished.

Ask: **If Christ is the center of God's plan, and God's will is to bring everything under Christ's headship, what's our role in these plans?**

After you've worked your way through the Ephesians passage, talk about questions three and four in Section III, page 80 in the journal. One main idea of this passage is that the knowledge of God's will means godly living and good works—which is what Ephesians 2:10 states.

Do you agree that God's will is more about how we live than what we do? Does this change the way you think about God's will for your life? Explain.

Group members might want to refer to the situations listed in question five in the journal. For example, it really isn't a question of finding God's will or missing it. It's all about a relationship with Him, and a desire to please Him.

Explain that God gives His people a lot of freedom. Ask group members to describe their decision-making processes. **Who do you talk to and what other things do you consider when you have to make a decision?** Brainstorm together to come up with different examples that help people make decisions.

Reflect and Respond

Check with group members to see if they have any more questions concerning God's will. Read this quote from Saint Augustine and ask group members for their reactions: **Love God and do as you please.**

Explain that the more people love God, the more they will do what pleases Him. Christians can't do whatever they want, because the Bible has set limits on their actions and choices. But as they grow in their relationships with Jesus, the choices they make will be consistent with a godly lifestyle.

■3 Sharing and Prayer

Focus your sharing on decisions group members need to make. Spend a few minutes praying for each other about these decisions; then close in prayer, repeating some of the requests in Paul's prayer in Colossians 1:9-12. Don't forget to open it up to general sharing of requests and praises. Remind group members to complete Week Ten in time for your next group meeting.

Note: Before your next meeting, you'll need to ask another group member to help you out with a little project. It's probably a good idea if both of you come a bit early to the small group next week.

WEEK ◀10 In His Majesty's Service!

Being a Servant

Overview

- To show group members the high priority God places on serving others.
- To encourage group members to follow Jesus' example of servanthood.
- To motivate people to carry out their plans for serving others.

Scripture: Mark 10:35-45; Philippians 2:5-11

1 Getting Started

Housekeeping

Touch base with the group member who's helping out with the serving experiment (see Focus), so he or she knows what to do. That person could even volunteer to make any announcements for you. Keep this up until you debrief the group in Focus.

With this meeting, you will finish the second unit in this book. Decide as a group if you want a week off or if you want to move right into the third unit. Set a time for your next meeting. If you decide to go ahead with the third unit, tell your group members to prepare for it by reading Week Eleven, which is titled "What (On Earth) Are You Doing?"

Icebreaking

Give group members a couple of minutes to think of a commercial that describes how they felt this week. When people are ready, have each member sing or say the commercial's jingle or catch line, and then explain why it describes his or her week. Or if your group is close, other members could guess why the person chose the ad. Another way to do this is to divide the group into two teams and compete to come up with the most advertising jingles in three minutes.

Ask: **What do you think these ads say about what our culture values? Do you think this is an accurate assumption? Why or why not?**

Opening

Say something such as this: **Some people say you're stooping low when you serve others, but God says just the opposite about servanthood.**

Use this prayer or adapt it as you begin the Bible study.

God, help us understand what You said in Your Word about serving others, and to move beyond our personal selfishness as well as cultural selfishness and follow Jesus' example of servanthood. In Jesus' name. Amen.

2 Bible Study

Focus

Before the meeting, ask another group member to help you out with a little project. Explain that you want him or her to show the rest of the group what it means to be a servant.

As other group members arrive, this person should go out of his or her way to serve them. He could offer to bring in a chair for someone, take another person's coat and hang it up, get refreshments for people, refill drinks, and so on. Get creative with this one. Tell your cohort to act as natural as possible.

Use your "servant" as an example of what it means to serve. Ask: **Did you feel uncomfortable being served? Why or why not? When was the last time someone actually served you?**

Make the point that the reason that it was so odd to have someone act this way is because we're not used to seeing people actually serve others.

Dig In

Ask group members to turn to page 86 in their journals, and explain how they summarized Mark 10:35-37 (question one, Section II, "Glory-Bound Glory Hounds"). James and John wanted power and prestige.

What was right about James and John's thinking? What was wrong with it?

Have group members look up Mark 10:35-45 and find clues about James

INSIDE INSIGHTS

■ When Jesus asked James and John if they could drink the cup He drinks, Jesus used a Jewish expression that meant to share someone's fate.

■ Both James and John did suffer and die for Jesus. In fact, James is considered the first Christian martyr when he was put to death by Herod in Acts 12:2. Church tradition believes that John was immersed in a caldron of boiling oil, but survived. He was eventually banished to the island of Patmos where he proceeded to write the Book of Revelation.

■ When a king sat on his royal throne, the places of honor were at his right and at his left.

■ In Matthew 20:21, it looks as if James and John's mother wanted her sons to ask Jesus to do whatever they wanted.

■ A ransom (Mark 10:45) was originally the price paid for the release of a slave. When Jesus died on the cross, He paid the price for our sins, releasing us from sin's bondage.

and John's attitude. They were right about their thinking regarding Jesus' being seated in glory on the Father's throne. There was plenty wrong about James and John's attitude. For example, they were arrogant, self-centered, and ignorant about Jesus' purpose in coming to earth.

Talk about Jesus' reply in Mark 10:38-40 (question three in Section II).

What do you think Jesus meant when He talked about drinking from the same cup He drank from and being baptized with the same baptism?

Explain what the expression "drinking from the same cup" meant (see the information in the Inside Insights section). You could also ask someone to read Mark 9:31, 32, where Jesus predicts His death. He was referring to His suffering and death.

Do you think Jesus was predicting suffering and death for James and John in verse 40? Why or why not?

Using their responses to questions five, six, and seven in Section II, "Glory-Bound Glory Hounds," as a basis for the discussion, ask group members these questions.

What was Jesus' purpose for coming to earth? (Mark 10:45 says it all.) **How could true greatness come from serving others? What's so radical about what Jesus said in Mark 10:43, 44?**

Get group members to contrast the Gentile leaders' attitudes with Jesus' attitude. Jesus basically turned the values and attitudes of the world upside down. Also, have people pull in their comments on Philippians 2:3, 4.

Ask: **What's the stereotype of a humble person?**

For example, a weak-willed, wimpy sort of person. In olden days, this kind of person was described as a milquetoast, based on Caspar Milquetoast, a comic strip character back in the 1930s. Caspar was timid, meek, and unassertive.

Point out that considering others better than yourselves doesn't mean that everyone else is superior to you, but you choose to make others look good and promote them instead of promoting yourself.

How did Jesus demonstrate that a humble person is just the opposite of a milquetoast kind of person?

Group members may want to show their diagrams, tracing Jesus' downward mobility in Philippians 2:6-8. Jesus didn't selfishly hang onto His equality with God, but chose to make Himself nothing. Jesus became a servant, and humbled Himself to the point of death. Jesus chose to become human and to serve others.

Because in God's kingdom true greatness comes through service, ask someone to read Philippians 2:9-11, which describes Christ's exaltation.

How can we follow Christ's radical example of service in practical ways?

 As a group, share your ideas for serving others from the passages in Section IV, "Just Do It." A couple of these passages show that serving others is meeting more than just a person's physical needs.

Here are some ideas for service.

• Matthew 5:38-42. You could decide not to insist on your way just because it's your right. Or, you could do more than what's asked (or expected) of you in a situation—like that no-brainer part-time job you have.

• Acts 2:44, 45. Service involves taking care of people's tangible needs. If you have the resources to meet a person's needs, then you should do something about it.

• Romans 12:15. Sometimes serving others means supporting people emotionally and spiritually. When you rejoice with someone else's success, you're looking out for the person's interests as Philippians 2:4 states.

• James 2:15, 16. James, the writer of this letter, got straight to the point about meeting people's physical needs. When you serve people like this, it shows that your faith is alive. Serving others is faith in action.

• I John 3:16-18. Here's a way to love with actions and in truth. You can provide clothing for someone who is in need. And this is not just for people who are destitute. A family in your church who has a new baby may need clothes for that child. Or a friend at school might need clothes for a special event.

 ## Reflect and Respond

If you think the members would like to do a group service project, brainstorm some ways you could meet the needs of people in your church, at school, or in someone's neighborhood. Use some of the ideas in the "Keep In Mind" section of the journal to get you started. Once you have an idea, set a date and choose someone to contact the person (or people) you want to help.

There's a slight problem about serving others and looking out for their interests—it doesn't come naturally.

Read the following statements to the group, and ask members to think about the ones that are hard for them to do.

Is it hard for you to:

• put other people's interests ahead of your own, especially rejoicing with them when they succeed?
• help people financially?
• not always insist on your own way, even when you're right?
• support people emotionally and spiritually?

Discuss these questions:

• Is it harder for you to serve someone or to ask for help? Why?

• What would you say are the three biggest barriers to serving others?

• What are the three biggest benefits?

To close, ask group members to turn to Philippians 2:5-11. Go around the group, taking turns reading this wonderful passage aloud.

3 Sharing and Prayer

Spend a minute or two in silent prayer, asking God for His help in serving others. Encourage group members to be a servant to someone this next week. You won't ask anyone for a report, but if someone wants to brag on another group member's servant spirit, that's okay.

As a group, share specific needs of people you know as well as group members' personal needs; then close in a time of prayer. Talk about the way God has answered prayer and the things for which people are thankful.

Leader's Tip: *Sharing prayer requests shouldn't become a buzz word for gossip. No one needs to know every single detail of every situation. Encourage group members to give enough information so people know what they're praying for, but not so much information it encourages gossip and speculation.*

WEEK 11 What (On Earth) Are You Doing?

Becoming a World-Changer

Overview

• Gain a perspective on the urgency and importance of Jesus' command to spread the Gospel.

• Learn how to live as "aliens and strangers" (I Peter 2:11).

• Understand what the future holds for believers and unbelievers.

• Understand what qualifies Jesus to be the only hope for humanity.

Scripture: Matthew 28:18-20 and selected Scripture passages

1 Getting Started

Housekeeping

Welcome any new people. Warmly and briefly explain to them the purpose of the study. Have current group members explain something they've learned during the study that's made a difference in their lives.

Discuss whether the current meeting time and place is still okay for the group. Make changes as needed. Encourage more people to get involved in leadership during this last unit since they've had plenty of time to observe how it's done. Make any other announcements that are necessary.

Icebreaking

Week 11, Section I in the disciple's journal lists the last words of some famous people. Ask your group members to come up with their own profound or humorous last words. As you distribute paper and markers, ask: **What do you think your last words might be? What do you think you will try to communicate?**

Encourage people to give their last words a creative title and to add an artistic touch if they want.

When everyone is done, gather all the sheets and randomly redistribute them. Have each person read one sheet aloud; then let people guess who wrote those last words. Give people time to explain the meaning behind their words. Afterward, discuss how powerful and important last words can be.

Opening

Say: **Some people's last words summarize their lifelong beliefs. Let's take a moment now to reaffirm our own beliefs by reciting the Apostle's Creed. You'll find it on page 142 in the Extra Stuff section at the back of your journal. Let's read it as our prayer to begin this study.**

The Apostle's Creed

I believe in God the Father Almighty, Maker of heaven and earth:

And in Jesus Christ His only Son, our Lord, who was conceived by the Holy Ghost, born of the Virgin Mary, suffered under Pontius Pilate, was crucified, dead, and buried; He descended into hell; the third day He rose again from the dead; He ascended into heaven and sitteth on the right hand of God the Father Almighty; from thence He shall come to judge the quick and the dead.

I believe in the Holy Ghost, the holy Christian [catholic] Church, the communion of saints, the forgiveness of sins, the resurrection of the body, and the life everlasting. Amen.

2 Bible Study

Focus

Tell this true story before discussing the perspectives of the famous people whose last words are printed in the disciple's journal, Section I.

Harvey Weinstein knows what perspective is. The 68-year-old millionaire tuxedo maker from New York City was kidnapped and placed in a tiny hole in the ground where he spent twelve days and nights. During that time, he fought insanity by remembering the things in his life that were important to him—all the way back to age six. In his isolation, he lost hope many times, thinking that he would never be found again, and would never get to see his family again. But after twelve days, he felt the touch of a New York City detective who reached down into that hole. His first thought was, "I knew God had smiled down on me." Harvey gained a little perspective on life during his stay in "Hell's Hole." He sees everything now in a different light.

Let group members react to the story. Then ask them to talk about any drastic change in perspective they have personally experienced.

Discuss the "Last Words Are Honest!" statements on page 95 in their journals. Find out which ones intrigued them most and why. Also find out which statements they most identified with and why.

Let them talk about how they think Jesus' final words in Matthew 28:18-20 differ from all the others.

Leader's Tip: Many Christians have experienced doubts about their eternal destination. Acknowledge that there may be people in the group who are dealing with doubts right now and who may identify with the fear expressed by O. Henry or the doubts expressed by Thomas Hobbes in the "Last Words" statements. Encourage those people to continue to work through their doubts and to seek godly counsel as needed.

Dig In

I suspect that most people spend very little time thinking about how short their lives really are. If they did, they would realize that their time on this earth is just a dot on the line of eternity.

People who realize how short life is often become motivated to make their brief stay on earth count for something. They begin to get a sense of what is really important in life.

Discuss the answers group members came up with for question one in Section II on page 97 in the disciple's journal. Supplement their ideas with selected comments from the Inside Insights section.

Invite a few volunteers to reveal their answers to question two in the disciple's journal about their life purpose. Get them to explain how their life purpose was shaped. What events or people influenced them?

Just before discussing question three, say something like this: **Suppose we end up spending eighty-five years here on earth. That's a long time. But is it very long compared to eight hundred years? How about eight thousand years? Eight million years? Eight billion years?!**

A good way to help earthly things, such as the desire for wealth or personal achievement, recede in importance is to compare the length of our

earthly lifetimes to our eternal lifetimes. When we know that we will be enjoying God's presence for eternity, is it worth it to freak when we miss out on the job we expected, the new car we wanted, or invitations to the "right" parties? Even though many of these things are important to us now, they actually are insignificant in light of eternity.

This doesn't mean we should never pursue some of those things. But knowing how short life is can motivate us to put our greatest time and efforts into the things that last forever.

Supplement your discussion about question four with this question: **How different might a Christian's response be to question four, compared to that of someone who doesn't know God?**

Explain that the six-month limit in question four is like the two-minute warning in a football game, when players sometimes experience renewed energy and focus.

Everyone will live forever; it's just a question of where. Scripture tells us that there are only two destinations—heaven or hell.

Find out what group members discovered about eternity in questions one and two of Section III (page 98 in the journal). Supplement their discoveries with the following comments.

For unbelievers:

• Luke 16:23—Jesus describes hell as "torment." Imagine unending, heightened physical pain combined with the emotional torment of depression, anxiety, fear, guilt, and every other possible emotional trauma. Now multiply that level of pain a "kazillion" times or so and we can begin to get an idea of what hell will be like.

• Revelation 21:8—Jesus uses strong descriptive words to paint a realistic picture of people who will experience the second death. Point out that death is two-fold—both physical and spiritual. Find out what people think the "second death" means. Everyone has to die once, which is the physical death as we know it. But not everyone has to experience the second death. Believers will escape it.

For believers:

• Matthew 5:10-12—God promises to reward those who are persecuted for being witnesses for Christ. Paul reminds us that all who live godly lives will suffer persecution (II Timothy 3:12). So what awaits those who are witnesses for Him is not just any reward; according to Jesus, it's a "great" reward!

• II Corinthians 5:9, 10—Paul says that our goal should be to please the Lord. It pleases God when we tell others about the love of Christ. One more motivation to do this is knowing that we will stand before God one day to be given rewards based on what we've done.

As you discuss questions three and four in Section III, explain that the word for the judgment seat of Christ is from the word "bema" [BAY-mah]. This word would have been familiar to Paul's Corinthian readers. Corinth hosted Olympic-type games at which a judge sat on a bema or stone platform. From that platform the judge made sure competitors followed the rules, and he could disqualify those who didn't. This same judge awarded the winners. He would take an olive wreath (called a "stephanos," or crown), which was woven into a semicircle, and place it on the head of a victor.

It is important to point out to your group that Paul is speaking of being judged in order to receive rewards, not to see who gets into heaven!

 See how many ways your group can think of how people believe one gets to heaven. Add them up. Vote for the most ridiculous-sounding one and the most believable one.

Briefly review answers to questions two, three, and four in Section IV. Then say: **These three statements don't leave room for anyone else to claim to be the Savior and hope for all humanity. Paul lists just one of the reasons Jesus is qualified to be the Savior—"who gave himself as a ransom for all"** (I Timothy 2:6).

Once, a man who was starting a new religion came to the great French statesman Charles de Talleyrand complaining that he could not make any converts. "What would you suggest I do?" he asked.

"I should recommend," said Talleyrand, "that you get yourself crucified, and then die, but be sure to rise again the third day."

Only Jesus died for sin. Only Jesus rose again. So only Jesus deserves to be called Savior.

Reflect and Respond

Ask: **What opportunities do you have right now to tell others about God?**

Give group members a few minutes or so to make their own lists of every relative, friend, and acquaintance who needs to hear the Gospel. Once their lists are completed, acknowledge that they may feel overwhelmed by the length. Encourage them to come up with ideas on how to make their task more manageable. List those ideas somewhere for all to see. Remind group members that the responsibility for the salvation of all these people does not rest on their shoulders but on God's. They merely need to make themselves available to be used by God to plant the seed.

Encourage group members to choose two people from their lists to focus on. Have them plan a good way to approach these individuals with the Gospel. Have group members pair up to give each other feedback about their ideas.

As a group, you might want to talk about past experiences with witnessing. This could alert people to pitfalls and successes that others have experienced.

3 Sharing and Prayer

Isaiah 49:6 has been referred to as the "great commission of the Old Testament." Set the tone for your prayer time by reading it aloud. Encourage people to pray aloud for the individuals God has placed in their lives who need to hear the Gospel. Complete the prayer time by asking God to tear down any obstacles that may be preventing group members from witnessing.

Remind group members to complete Week Twelve in the journal for your next group meeting.

WEEK ◄12► It's Not Always Easy

Living as a Witness for Christ

Overview

• Understand what hypocrites are and why God is against them.

• Challenge group members to live a blameless lifestyle, and by doing so attract others to Christ.

Scripture: Matthew 6:2, 5, 16; 7:1-5; 23:13-33 and other selected passages

1 Getting Started

Housekeeping

Take care of announcements. Find out if group members would like to make any changes regarding the small group in these last few weeks.

Icebreaking

Before your group meets, see if you can get your hands on a fake item such as imitation salt, a fake diamond or fur, a leather-look wallet or purse, etc.

Display the object and ask if group members can tell whether it is genuine or not. Let them touch, smell, or taste the item as needed and explain why they think it is fake or real. You might also want to display the real version of the item. Ask volunteers to describe the similarities and differences between the counterfeit and the real thing.

Ask: **What similarities are there between phony items and phony people?** Get group members' responses.

Opening

To set the tone for this group time, sing a song about sincere Christian living, such as "I Have Decided" (Michael Card, © 1981 Whole Armor Publishing Co., and Singspiration Music/ASCAP). Amy Grant sang it on her *Age to Age* album, available on both cassette and CD.

Have someone open in prayer. Here's a prayer you might want to use or adapt.

Heavenly Father, it's amazing that such a powerful and perfect God wants to use us to tell others about Your gift of salvation. Help us see witnessing as a privilege. And help us live in a way that attracts others to You. Help us be pure and blameless. In Jesus' name we pray. Amen.

2 Bible Study

Focus

One reason people give for rejecting Jesus and His church is "all those hypocrites who act like Christians on Sunday and live like everyone else the rest of the week." Do you think this is a fair statement? Why or why not?

Have group members turn to Week twelve, "It's Not Always Easy" (page 103 in the journal). As a group, talk about which phrases you agreed with or disagreed with (in the Section I chart) and why. Discuss whether group members' opinions are based on biblical principles, specific verses, or personal opinion.

If you agree, for instance, that Christians should talk differently from non-Christians, and if you are a Christian who, shall we say, occasionally has a "potty-mouth," does that make you a hypocrite? What I'm really trying to point out is that it is easy to act like a hypocrite. This is why more people

are not convinced of the reality of Christ when they look at the lives of many Christians.

So how can our lives actually be a witness for Christ? To answer, let's begin by looking at Jesus' encounter with the hypocrites of His day.

Before moving on, have the group come up with a concise definition of hypocrisy. Webster describes it succinctly: "[pretending] to be what one is not or to believe what one does not."

Leader's Tip: Some of the statements in the chart in Section I of the disciple's journal should spark quite a discussion because they encourage a difference of opinion. Make sure group members hear each other out before jumping in with their own comments. Remind them not to take differences of opinion personally.

Dig In

Before you go on, communicate some of the background information about Pharisees as explained in the Inside Insights section.

Find out what people wrote in their "Area of Hypocrisy" charts at the beginning of Section II in the disciple's journal. To help group members understand why Jesus reacted so negatively to the hypocrites of His day, ask: **Have you ever crossed paths with a hypocrite? What kind of impact did this person have on your life?**

Most people are likely to say that it was a negative experience and that they were probably hurt in the process; they may have felt betrayed by someone who said one thing and did another.

Jesus was pretty hard on the Pharisees because they influenced a lot of people. Think of all the ways Pharisees could make an impact in their society. Hint: Don't forget that the Pharisees were from the middle class. Get someone to list on the board key words concerning the Pharisees' impact.

Seek responses to question three in Section II of the disciple's journal.

3. Describe all the ways that various Pharisees might have reacted to Jesus' scathing words. How do you think you would have reacted if you were one of them?

If the Pharisees were like people today, and they probably were, some of them were likely to react negatively to criticism. Some may have felt miffed, angry, filled with hate, or wanted vengeance against such an upstart as Jesus, a mere carpenter's son. Others may have admitted that Jesus made a good point but took no action; others may have seen the need to take stock of their lives and their relationship with God.

Help students see that they might be able to accurately determine their reaction to Jesus' criticism based on how they have reacted to God's discipline in the past.

Let's read about another aspect of hypocrisy in the lives of the Pharisees.

Have someone read Matthew 7:1-5 aloud while the rest of the group reads along silently.

If you had to sum up Jesus' criticism in this passage in one sentence and in contemporary terms, how would you say it?

Here are two examples of what group members might say: You can spot a sin in someone else's life from a mile away, but you use a different standard when you evaluate yourselves. Or: Get your own act together before you point your judgmental fingers at anyone else.

■ One of Jesus' greatest frustrations was dealing with the Pharisees. They taught that the oral law, regulated by religious leaders, was as important as the Old Testament law and equally inspired. Outwardly they appeared pious; inside they were dead. According to the *New Bible Commentary: Revised*, "They were not necessarily insincere, but they had such a wrong idea of what religion was about that their usually correct outward acts did not correspond to any inward spiritual reality."

■ Matthew 6:2, 5, 16—Some commentators say these Pharisees actually had trumpet players blow their horns to call attention to their giving. They would also go to the busiest street corner to pray so that they could be seen by others. And they would let everyone know how spiritual they were when fasting by the gloomy look on their faces.

■ Acts 16:16-34—Paul and Silas were unjustly arrested, stripped to the waist, and beaten with wooden rods that were usually made of birchwood and were about 18 inches long (like a police officer's billy club). Ouch! Verse 23 tells us they were "severely flogged." Then they were thrown into prison, not just any old prison cell, but the "inner cell" (vs. 24). This room was usually reserved for the worst of criminals (murderers, thieves, etc.).

4. Why do you think hypocrites make God so angry?

Allow group members to express a variety of opinions here. Apparently, God is very touchy about spiritual leaders who point people away from the truth, whether they do it knowingly or unknowingly.

Leader's Tip: Always encourage group members to back up their answers or opinions, whenever possible, with Scripture. This is helpful when they answer questions like number four, which encourages them to try to answer from someone else's point of view.

Reflect and Respond

Do you think Jesus' words to these hypocrites apply to us today? Then say: **Acting is fine in television, film, and theater, but it has no place in the church. God wants you to avoid hypocrisy like the plague, and instead, He wants you to . . . ?**

Write the last sentence on the board so people can finish the sentence themselves. Get group members' responses. Their answers will lead into the questions in Section III of the disciple's journal.

Talk about what God means when He says that He wants His people to live a blameless lifestyle. Find out how people responded to questions one and two in their journals.

Have everyone take a look at Philippians 2:14, 15, in which Paul equates being blameless with being pure and without fault. Write the following information on the board so that group members can see the contrast between people who are sinful and people who are blameless.

Blameless people are:
- pure
- children of the Lord
- without fault
- morally straight
- shining His light

Sinful people are:
- guilty
- immoral
- children of the devil
- full of sin
- morally crooked
- full of darkness, depraved

Notice Paul uses the illustration of stars shining in the universe. What a contrast! Contrast is why jewelers display diamonds against a dark velvet

backdrop. Our being blameless is contrasted against the dark backdrop of a sinful world.

Explain the difference between "blameless" and "sinless." We have all sinned, so our track record is blemished. But we can be blameless right now! To be blameless means our lives point others to Christ.

 3. If we grant that Christians do sin, how can a Christian realistically live blamelessly in God's eyes?

After you get a couple of responses to this question, point out any similarities there may be with the sentence completions they finished earlier. To spark more ideas about how one can live blamelessly before God, have people look at all the verses referred to in question four.

Refer to the information about Paul and Silas when you deal with question five. Point out that they went through all this. They were:

falsely accused (vss. 20, 21)   thrown into prison (vs. 23)
publicly humiliated (vs. 22)   thrown into maximum security (vs. 24)
arrested (vs. 22)   locked into painful stocks (vs. 24)
stripped (vs. 22)   guarded carefully by a Roman soldier (vs. 24)
severely beaten with rods (vs. 22)

What a day! How would you respond to circumstances like this? Would you cry? call a lawyer? fight back? give up? question God? curse the crowd? defend yourself? blame it on Silas? etc.

Let people answer before moving on.

Have you ever wondered why a Christian's lifestyle can be such a powerful testimony? Here are a few convincing reasons:

1. Your lifestyle can be powerful because others are watching—not the CIA or the FBI, but the CNC (Curious Non-Christians). Younger kids at church are watching, too. Your boss is watching. Your coach is watching. Strangers are watching. Your friends may not hear any Sunday sermons, but they see sermons Monday through Saturday. What are you preaching?

2. Your lifestyle can be a powerful testimony to God when you face problems and crises in God's strength. Christians experience the same problems as others do—a family member may become seriously ill or die, you may

get a flat tire, sit out of the game on the bench, get acne, flunk a test. But when you depend on God during the crises, those who don't know Christ may see their need to depend on Him too.

3. God can use your lifestyle to persuade someone of the truth. It's a fact that what you say, what you do, and your character are powerful statements of the reality of your faith. Jesus said when you shine your light in this way, men will see it and ultimately glorify your Father in heaven (Matthew 5:16).

3 Sharing and Prayer

Invite a volunteer to read Jude 24 aloud. Follow up with comments like these:

How will we make it? How will we remain blameless? Through Jesus.

• **Jesus will keep you from falling as you trust in Him.**

• **Jesus will present you blameless some day, without fault, to the Father.**

• **Jesus will do this for you with great joy.**

The key, once again, is using God's resources and not our own.

 Have group members find a partner to discuss their comments concerning the personal assessments they were to make in question six. Have them pray for each other's positive and negative areas of blamelessness.

Gather people back together to remind them of the following:

Christians are to be different in these areas: values, lifestyle, friendships, moral purity, life purpose, source of strength, ability to handle problems, forgiveness, our eternal destiny, etc.

Close by having everyone read Jude 24 in unison.

Challenge group members to spend at least five minutes a day in prayer for the next seven days concerning the things they described in the "negatives" column in the chart under question six. Remind everyone to complete Week Thirteen for next week's small group time.

WEEK 13 The Truth Hurts

Understanding God's Good News —Part 1

Overview

• To realize that an understanding of people's sinfulness is essential to the Gospel.

• To clearly communicate the basics of the Gospel, including the bad news about sin and its penalty.

• To encourage group members to feel more comfortable in talking about sin.

Scripture: Psalm 103:8-12; Romans 1:28-31; 3:10-12, 23; Ephesians 2:1-3; and selected passages about sin and God's holiness

1 Getting Started

Housekeeping

This would be a good time to get together with your other small group leaders and choose the next topic in the discipleship series, *The Main Thing*. This is also a good time to encourage more people to become involved in group leadership, and perhaps give current leaders a bit of a break. Check with group members to see if the small group meeting times still work for them.

Icebreaking

Read each either/or statement, then have group members raise their hands to vote for the situation they feel is worse than the other.

• Being called on by the teacher and not knowing the answer OR getting a low grade on a pop quiz.

• Breaking up with the person you've been dating OR not have a boyfriend or girlfriend at all.

• Looking for work OR being laid off.

• Living with parents who fight constantly OR having a parent move out of the house.

Be sure to give group members a chance to explain their choices. Also talk about the different reactions people have to bad news and stressful situations. The point of this icebreaker is that no one likes bad news, but once you deal with it, you can move on and resolve the situation. That's why you have to talk about the bad news of sin, before you talk about the good news of salvation and God's forgiveness of sin.

Or, begin on a lighter note by creating a funny add-on story, where things go from bad to worse. Get the story going with this short beginning: **Anthony's old girlfriend is in town. His current girlfriend, Mariah, is out of town. Not having one of those possessive-type relationships, Anthony figures Mariah would want him to see his old girlfriend. So he decides to meet the old girlfriend for lunch. And that's where things begin to go downhill.** To move on to the next person, people may use this transition: "You'd think things couldn't get much worse, but they did"; then the next person picks up the story.

Opening

Read aloud Psalm 103:8-12, a beautiful hymn about God's compassion and love for His sinful people. This psalm provides a contrast to the topic of sin, and will remind group members that there's a solution to sin—God's forgiveness and grace. Here's the psalm:

The Lord is compassionate and gracious, slow to anger, abounding in love. He will not always accuse, nor will he harbor his anger forever; he does not treat us as our sins deserve or repay us according to our iniquities. For as high as the heavens are above the earth, so great is his love for those

who fear him; as far as the east is from the west, so far has he removed our transgressions from us.

2 Bible Study

Focus

Give group members this true-false quiz about sin. People may jot down their answers in the margins of their journals or on a scrap piece of paper.

Decide if the following statements are true or false.

1. Some sins are worse than others.

2. What was considered a sin ten years ago may not be a sin today.

3. Christians don't intentionally sin.

4. If a sin doesn't hurt anyone, it's not really a sin.

5. One way or another, we pay for our sins.

Instead of giving the right answers, have group members explain their choices, using Scripture to support their answers. This will help all of you to clarify your thinking about what sin is.

Move into the next section by saying something like this: **If we want people to come to Christ, we need to know what we're talking about. The next two weeks, we're going to investigate the Gospel, the good news of salvation that's found in the cross of Jesus Christ.**

Ask group members to explain their responses to questions one and two in Section I, "The Gospel Truth" (page 111), in the disciple's journal.

Based on group members' responses, come up with a definition of the Gospel. (For example, a working definition might be: "The Gospel is the good news of salvation offered through Jesus Christ.") If you'd like, write the definition in the space below; then at the end of next week's meeting, read it to the group and see if they want to change anything.

This week, you'll be talking about God's righteous standard, people's inability to meet that standard, and the penalty for sin. This will show why the bad news of the Gospel is so bad.

Leader's Tip: *As group members talk, watch people's eyes and call on quiet ones who are probably ready to contribute to the discussion but need a gentle boost to start talking.*

Dig In

Ask: **Even though we're Christians, why do you think we need to investigate the Gospel?**

Here are a few reasons why understanding the Gospel is important. Many people misrepresent the Gospel, by adding something to it (like works) or subtracting something from it (like repentance). You need to know exactly what the Gospel is and what it isn't.

You'll better understand your own salvation. Your appreciation for God's work in your life will increase as your understanding of the Gospel increases. To know the Gospel better is to know Jesus better.

You can't share what you don't know. In order to be effective witnesses for Jesus Christ, you need to know not just the "what" of the Gospel, but the "why" as well.

As a group, come up with a concise definition of sin. For example: sin can be active—committing a specific sin; it can be passive—neglecting to do something you ought to do; and sin can be an attitude or an action. But sin is always disobeying God.

We all have different images of what a sinner is. Some people think of sinners as derelicts and murderers, and others view sinners as people who never go to church on Sunday. The real question asks: "What does God say a sinner is?"

Go around the group, and ask people to describe a sinner, based on their responses to question one in Section II, "The Root Problem," page 112. It's won't be a pretty sight.

Ask different people to look up Romans 1:28-31; 3:10-12, 23; and Ephesians 2:1-3 in their Bibles.

Take a couple of minutes to discuss question two in Section II. **What image comes to mind when you hear the phrase "fall short"?**

INSIDE

Feel free to add the comment from Inside Insights about how sin means missing the mark. Basically, we don't measure up to what God intended us to be before the Fall, before sin.

As you read these descriptions of humanity, what jumped out at you? (For example, gossips and people who disobey their parents are lumped together with those who "committed indecent acts with other men" and murderers. Or there is no one who does good and what is right. The description of people in Romans 3:10-12 is downright depressing.)

Do you think this is an accurate description of humankind? Why or why not?

■ In the first century, when a country conquered its enemy, the army would come marching triumphantly back home. A victory celebration would follow, with joy and singing filling the city streets. The festivities would last for days. Why? Because good news had arrived with the victorious army.

■ In archery, when the archer misses the bull's-eye, he or she has literally "missed" the mark. That's where the concept of sin in the Bible comes from. To sin is to "miss the mark" of God's perfect standard—His holy character. Paul is saying we have missed God's "bull's-eye" of holiness by our sinful nature and our sinful actions.

As a group, list some contrasts between God's character and people's characters; between God's view of humankind and people's view of themselves. Group members may want to refer to journal questions three and four in Section II and questions one and two in Section III, "The Grim Solution."

Mention these points as you look for the contrasts between God and humans. Isaiah 6:3 is a declaration of God's character: He is holy. The "holy, holy, holy" repetition stresses God's infinite holiness. Because of God's holy nature, He can't look on sin with approval or tolerate it (see Habakkuk 1:13a).

What does it mean that God is holy? (God is perfect and distinct from us. He's above us. God is the Creator; we are the creation. God's character is infinitely perfect in every way. He cannot tolerate sin in His presence.)

The Bible makes two assumptions about us and our sin. The first assumption is that sin is directed against God, and the second is that we can't do

anything by ourselves to change our essential character or act differently from it.

How do these two basic assumptions affect our goodness and even our good works? (According to Isaiah 64:6, our good works are "like filthy rags.") Point out that even the best of our good works don't measure up to God's standard of holiness.

Does this mean that non-Christians can't do good things? Why or why not? (Actually, non-Christians can do good things because all people have been created in God's image. See Acts 10:1, 2, 34, 35. The real issue is that we're sinners, God is holy, and no amount of good deeds can close the gap between God and us.)

Think of it this way. It's like God is on one side of a massive canyon and we are on the other. The bad news is that there isn't a soul on earth who can reach the other side. Many have tried, but they just end up at the bottom of the canyon.

Talk about question three and the fact that sin originates in our hearts and minds.

Talk about question five in Section III, "The Grim Solution." Talk about the contrasts Jesus made in these two passages.

 5. You can probably hear the protest, "I don't think a loving God would ever send anyone to hell." Read John 3:17, 18 and 5:24. According to Jesus, what's the difference between people who die and are separated from God's presence and people who die and are with God?

Does a loving God send people to hell? Explain your answer.

(People end up in hell because of a conscious choice they make to reject God's truth as revealed supremely in Jesus. Because God is righteous and just, He must punish sin. God will be fair as He administers His justice. Sometimes our human justice system breaks down, punishing the innocent and rewarding the guilty. But God is not like that. He is always just.)

Reflect and Respond

This probably has been a fairly serious small group meeting. Because of that, give group members a chance to express how they feel about this week's emphasis on the bad news of the Gospel. They may want to explain what they checked for question seven in Section III of the disciple's journal.

When everyone has had a chance to talk, say something such as this:

What basic points would you try to emphasize about sin if you were talking to someone? (See page 115 in the journal, question five, Section III.)

1. God is holy and perfect. He is without sin and can't tolerate wickedness.
2. We are all sinners. We fail to measure up to God's righteous standard.
3. Because God is holy and just, He must punish sin. God would cease to be God if He let one single sin go unpunished.

News, even bad news, has to be announced. Okay, this is another way of saying that we have to witness to people, but it doesn't have to be a big ordeal. Get your group to think of witnessing as telling their personal stories of how they came to Jesus.

Take the time to tell your stories to each other, using what you wrote down in questions five and six in Section II, "The Root Problem" (page 113 in the journal). You'll not only get practice in witnessing, but also get to know each other even better as you listen to each other's stories of faith.

3 Sharing and Prayer

Close by praying for friends and family members who don't know Jesus. Ask your group members if they're ready for some good news after studying this chapter. Assure them that the next week will bring them that good news. Remind them to complete Week Fourteen for your next group meeting.

WEEK 14 A Message of Love

Understanding God's Good News —Part 2

Overview

- To help group members clearly understand what Jesus did on the cross.
- To give people practice in sharing their salvation stories.
- To increase members' appreciation for their salvation.

Scripture: Romans 5:1, 2; II Corinthians 5:21; I Peter 2:22-24; I John 2:2

1 Getting Started

Housekeeping

Spend a few minutes talking about what comes next for the group. Are there people who want to become involved in leadership? What should be the next group study? If you haven't already done so, try *Never the Same*, another study in the series, which is about knowing God the Father, God the Son, and God the Holy Spirit.

Icebreaking

On your way out the door for this week's meeting, grab a small stack of newspapers or magazines you might have lying around.

For the icebreaker, have group members think of one good thing and one bad thing that happened to them this week. Have them design their own front page or magazine cover, announcing their news. Encourage creativity (and sensationalism!). When finished, take turns reading each other's covers.

Opening

To open, read the first verse to the old hymn, "The Old Rugged Cross."

On a hill far away stood an old rugged cross,
The emblem of suffering and shame;
And I love that old cross where the dearest and best
For a world of lost sinners was slain.

So I'll cherish the old rugged cross,
Till my trophies at last I lay down;
I will cling to the old rugged cross,
And exchange it some day for a crown.

Say something like this: **The hymn writer did a good job of expressing his appreciation and amazement for what Jesus did on the cross.**

2 Bible Study

Focus

Start by going over the main points of last week's meeting about the bad news of the Gospel:

1. God is holy and perfect. He is without sin and can't tolerate wickedness.

2. We are all sinners. We fail to measure up to God's righteous standard.

3. Because God is holy and just, He must punish sin. God would cease to be God if He let one single sin go unpunished.

Emphasize the importance of understanding these truths in order to tell someone else about the Gospel. You might also mention that a person might not completely understand everything about salvation when he or she first trusts Christ, but that's okay. God will help them become mature children of God.

As a group, describe your different comfort levels in talking about salvation (Section I, "As Good as It Gets," pages 119-120 in the journal). Be open with each other as you talk about the qualms you might have about witnessing. Try to get to the reasons why we Christians often feel uncomfortable talking about the greatest thing that has ever happened to us, our salvation.

Instead of picturing nameless masses who need to hear about God, encourage group members to think of one person they know who needs Jesus. Have them keep that person in mind during the small group meeting.

Leader's Tip: During the meeting, occasionally ask group members how the people they're thinking of would respond to the topic at hand. What questions would they have about Jesus' death on the cross? By doing this, you'll help each other clearly communicate the message of salvation.

Dig In

The goal of this meeting is to give people a basic understanding of Jesus' sacrifice on the cross, so they'll tell others about God's saving grace.

Have group members explain how they marked up the four passages in question two of Section II, "Cross Purposes" (see page 121 in the journal). For example, we marked up Romans 5:1, 2 like this:

Therefore, since we have been <u>justified</u> through faith, we have <u>peace with God</u> through our Lord Jesus Christ, through whom we have gained access by faith into this <u>grace</u> in which we now stand. And we rejoice in the <u>hope</u> of the glory of God.

Discuss some of the questions group members may have had about the passages. Rather than explaining every single word, we've chosen to comment on a few select phrases. There also are extra questions to throw out for discussion.

• The word "justified" in Romans 5:1, 2 has legal overtones. It means to acquit or to declare righteous. It's the opposite of "condemned." God is the one who releases us from the penalty of sin and treats us as righteous in Christ.

What do we gain from our justification? (We gain peace with God and access to Him.)

Get group members to explain what this means to them in everyday life. You might want to point out that our peace with God has more to do with an objective standing—we're no longer God's enemies—than it does with a subjective feeling of peace or calm.

• The phrase "made him who had no sin to be sin for us" in II Corinthians 5:21 is a decent summary of the Gospel. In Jesus' death, He took our place and literally took on the sins of humanity as He hung on the cross.

What do you think it must have been like for Jesus to become sin for us? (Jesus' cry from the cross, "My God, my God, why have you forsaken me?" [Mark 15:34], shows how deeply Jesus felt His abandonment by His Father as He bore the sins of humanity.)

• The phrases "bore our sins in his body" and "by his wounds you have been healed" in I Peter 2:24 mean sort of the same thing as II Corinthians 5:21. Jesus satisfied God's righteous demands.

• The key words in I John 2:2 are "atoning sacrifice." Add these comments to the ones in the disciple's journal. The idea behind the word "atonement" points to the process of bringing those who are estranged back to God. God has always provided the way back for people. In the Old Testament, sacrifices were God's appointed way of portraying atonement. In the New Testament, Jesus' death on the cross was the final and perfect sacrifice for sin.

Why was there a need for atonement? (Sin and people's inability to deal with sin made atonement necessary.)

When you've finished talking about the passages, say: **Describe the relationship between what Jesus did on the cross and what we gained by His death.** (It comes down to this: everything Jesus accomplished on the cross was for us. Because we were spiritually dead, Jesus had to do everything for us.)

If Jesus has done everything for us, what's our role?

As John 1:12, 3:16, Acts 3:19, and Romans 3:22 state, our role is to repent and believe in Jesus and what He accomplished on the cross. It has been said that many people miss heaven by a mere fourteen inches—the distance from their heads to their hearts.

Spend some time talking about questions two and three in Section III, "Believe It or Not," page 123 in the journal. Encourage each other to come up with clear explanations of what it means to trust Jesus for salvation. If people are up for it, have short roleplays, where one person plays the part of a non-Christian and the other is the Christian.

Repentance involves a change and a turning away from something (in this case, sin) to something—in this case, it's a Someone, Jesus.

Reflect and Respond

Spend several minutes sharing your salvation stories. Group members may read exactly what they wrote in their journals (see question three, Section IV, "Your Good News Story," page 124), or recap the major highlights of their stories.

If you'd like, agree as a group to memorize the verses listed in the "Keep In Mind" section: Romans 3:23; 6:23; 5:8; and Ephesians 2:8, 9.

3 Sharing and Prayer

INSIDE INSIGHTS

■ Here's a list of the theological terms that the group has been talking about:

• Justification—A legal term meaning to acquit or declare someone righteous. Because of Jesus' death on the cross, believers are declared righteous.

• Propitiation—This has the idea of appeasement. God is satisfied with Jesus' payment for sin. Jesus made payment to God, not Satan, for the penalty of our sin. God was the one who was wronged by our sin, not Satan.

• Atonement—Refers to the covering of sin through sacrifice.

• Substitution—Or representative. The death of a representative counts as the death of those He represents.

We don't recommend making these terms a part of everyday conversation, but they are worth knowing.

Close the group time with a short time of praise to Jesus for everything He accomplished on the cross. Go around the group and have members say sentence prayers of thanks, based on questions four and five in Section III in their journals. Also, challenge group members to pray next week for people they know who need to know Jesus.

Before people either head for the food or leave, remind them that next week is the last week in this disciple's journal, *No Turning Back.*

WEEK 15 Don't Keep the Faith!

Telling Your Friends about Jesus

Overview

• Examine the three main obstacles to witnessing and determine how to overcome them.

• Equip and challenge each group member to reach his or her world for Christ.

Scripture: II Timothy 1:7, 8; I Peter 3:15; Mark 1:40-45 and other selected verses

1 Getting Started

Housekeeping

By this time, you should have a pretty good idea about what it means to be a disciple of Jesus Christ. You ought to feel a sense of accomplishment for helping to take the group through this rewarding study.

Invite people to talk about the impact that the Bible study has had on their spiritual lives. Tell the group what impact it has had on you. Let the group know how much you appreciate everyone in it. You may also want to tell each group member what growth you have seen in his or her life. Thank people for their willingness to get serious about their faith.

Find out who is available to start another study, which book in the series they would like to work with next, and when and where. Also decide who will order and distribute the books.

If you have time, have a brief celebration at the end of this study to bring it to an end. Provide snacks, perhaps play some contemporary Christian music in the background, and let people linger as long as possible.

Icebreaking

This final icebreaker will enable group members to show their appreciation for each other. Write each person's name on a separate 3" x 5" card and put the cards in a small paper bag. Have each person pull one card out of the bag and write down a statement that will build up the person whose name was selected. It could be a comment about a virtue or character trait, or appreciation for something said or done during the course of the Bible study.

Optional: If you have the money and the time to shop for small items (tiny New Testaments, small picture frames, a single flower, etc.), display them on a table. Let each group member choose an item to present, along with the card, to the person whose name he or she drew. Tell him or her to try to find some connection between the item and the person. For example, a small picture frame could be presented to someone along with this statement: "I have learned something about Jesus from you during the course of this Bible study. You have shown me a new way to picture Jesus."

Allow time for people to present their cards and gifts.

Opening

Before launching into this final session on following Christ, prayerfully sing an appropriate song such as "Step by Step" by Rich Mullins (Edward Grant, Inc.).

2 Bible Study

Focus

Say: **Do you remember seeing news reports about the Olympic torch as it was carried from runner to runner in the weeks before the Summer Olympic games began? During the opening ceremonies, the final runner on the last leg of the trip entered the Olympic** stadium holding the flaming torch high. Thousands of spectators packed the grandstands in the stadium and millions from around the world watched on TV. The runner gracefully raced up the almost-vertical stairs, and at the top, used the small torch to light a huge Olympic torch. The flame was able to burn brightly for the duration of the Olympic games because all of the runners faithfully fulfilled their responsibility.

The Good News of Jesus Christ is like that Olympic torch. You are like the runners. The torch has been passed to you by someone else and now it is your turn to run your leg of the journey. Your unsaved friends could be the next runners if you faithfully run to them with the Gospel. The grandstands of heaven are packed. A great host is cheering you on. I am cheering you on. God is cheering you on. So don't let anyone or anything stop you from passing the torch.

INSIDE

■ To add to the discussion concerning the meaning of "power" in II Timothy 1:7, 8— God Himself empowers people to become His children and to make others part of His kingdom. (See the Holy Spirit's role in this in Acts 2.) Christ Himself is the power of God (I Corinthians 1:24). The word "power" in verse 7 is further identified as the "power of God" in verse 8.

■ II Timothy 1:7, 8—Notice in verse 8 that suffering can be associated with witnessing (the apostle Paul is writing this from prison). Despite the possibility (likelihood) of suffering, God wants believers to boldly spread the word about Him.

For the past several weeks, we have looked at how to have an eternal perspective on life, the importance of living a blameless lifestyle, and how to better communicate the Gospel. Now we are going to take a look at three obstacles to telling the world about our Savior. If we can overcome them, we can sprint toward the finish like champions in the faith. The three obstacles are fear, ignorance, and apathy.

Leader's Tip: *If you have time, try to familiarize yourself thoroughly with the Olympic information so that you don't have to read it word for word. Tell it enthusiastically.*

Dig In

Find out if someone came up with a really good made-up word for the fear of witnessing (question one). After you have a few laughs, get a little more serious by finding out what number people circled on the fear scale in Section II, question two. Ask them to explain their fears (question three).

Get them talking about the source of their fears by asking question four.

4. If our timidity (or fear) doesn't come from God, where do you think it comes from?

Point out that Satan is not the sole source of our fears, but that other factors come into play including the ones they may have acknowledged in question three. After having someone read II Timothy 1:7, 8 aloud, stress that Scripture tells us that God is not a source of our fears.

Help the group understand the terms power, love, and self-discipline in the context of II Timothy 1:7, 8 by having them list synonyms for each word. Then have them talk about how these words relate to witnessing. Here are a few samples of synonyms:

Power: authority, ability, strength, influence, control, invincibility

Love: affection, attachment, devotion, passion, ardor

Self-discipline: self-control, determination, resolve, unyielding

Ask: **Do any of these words describe you or your style when it comes to witnessing? How?**

As a group, see how many fear factors you can list when it comes to witnessing. Explain that many of those fears are natural, and some of them are justified. In other words, having a fear of being rejected or losing a friend is something that could actually happen. But where does this fear come from? And should we fear? Can we actually use fear to help us?

Ask group members where they think this fear comes from. Their answers might include the following: intimidation of people, the devil, the pressure of the world, or our own weak hearts. Tell them the Bible provides answers to overcoming our fears in the following verses:

• Psalm 118:6—One way to relieve fear is to remember the presence of God. Remind group members how some of them may have been afraid of the dark as children and how their mom or dad would come into their bedroom to comfort them and to be with them. Or talk about how their parents may have held their hand at the dentist or in the emergency room at the hospital. Just having mom or dad in the room could help to make everything all right. How much more so with God! He is with them. In fact, Jesus promised to be present with His disciples in a special way as they witnessed for Him (Matthew 28:20). So fears can be eased or overcome just knowing God is right there. Someone has said, "I'd rather walk in the dark with Jesus than walk in the light by myself."

• Matthew 10:28, 29—Jesus tells His disciples here not to be afraid of anyone (see Psalm 27:1, 2). The reason for this is that people can't hurt our souls (the real person inside each of us). They may laugh, criticize, or even attack us, but they can't really hurt us . . . so don't be afraid of them. There is only one we should properly fear. Jesus goes on in this passage to relieve our fears by talking about God's care for His children. In verses 32 and 33, He says that He will stand up for us in heaven if we stand up for Him here! There's some motivation! We don't be afraid of mere people who can't really hurt us.

• II Corinthians 5:10, 11—And speaking of motivation, the apostle Paul says that because he fears the Lord, he witnesses for Christ. But this fear is not the kind of fear we normally think of. He is not terrified of God because God is cruel. In the context of these verses, Paul fears that if he doesn't tell the world about Christ, he won't please the Lord (vs. 9). But he also fears he won't receive spiritual rewards from Christ (vs. 10). Another fear was that he would live his life without accomplishing something great for God (vs. 15). He was afraid his life would come to an end and not have anything to show for it. It's like wanting to do well on a test, so you study hard. You fear making a bad grade (or flunking it!), so you are motivated to do something about it. Or you fear losing the race, so you train harder. Your fears in that way can be good. So even though you don't need to live in some kind of legalistic fear of God, each of us should be motivated to share Christ by a healthy fear of:

  • not pleasing God,

  • not receiving rewards from Christ,

  • not living a life that's productive for Him.

So the only fear we should really have is not the fear of people, but the proper fear of God.

Reinforce these points by discussing the four additional helps for overcoming fear (see the end of Section II). Find out which ones were most helpful to group members.

Remember:

- **God is with you.**
- **No one can really hurt you and Christ will stand up for you one day.**
- **Have a healthy fear of missing out on reward's day!**

Now move on to Section III in the disciple's journal titled "Tongue Tied."

We know what we want to say, we have heard others explain the Gospel, but when it comes our turn to explain, it comes out wrong or confused.

Have everyone take a look at I Peter 3:15 and underline key words or concepts in the verse. Point out these words that are directly related to witnessing.

• *Be prepared.* Be alert by doing your homework and training for the witnessing event.

• *Give an answer.* This implies that you know what the answer is; which is why two previous chapters dealt with knowing and understanding the Gospel. You don't have to be gifted to explain the Gospel, you just need to know it. The Gospel is simple to understand and simple to learn. But our world is like a confusing mass of highways leading into a major metropolis with its many opinions about truth and religion. Your job is to guide unbelievers down the narrow path that leads them to the foot of the cross. You don't have to know all the deeper theological truths (like, How many angels can you fit on the head of a pin?). You just need to know the simple Gospel well. So be ready to give an answer.

• *Everyone who asks you.* It doesn't matter who they are, the Gospel is for them. They may be like you or different from you. They can be rich or poor, from another race or country, churched or unchurched. They can be homeless or a debutante. It doesn't matter. The bottom line is: They need salvation and you have the Gospel. And no matter what you might not have in common with them, at least you were once lost just as they are.

• *To give the reason.* Peter points out that our faith is not a fairy tale; it's a reality based on historical fact. Christianity is a reasonable faith. You don't give up your intellect when you become a Christian. Your faith is founded on documented facts such as these.

Jesus was born of a virgin.

He lived a sinless life.

He died on a Roman cross.

He rose again on the third day.

The Gospels give evidence that He is God and the only way to heaven.

What Peter is saying is that when we witness we aren't just saying, "Well, I know my faith is real because I feel it in my heart. I just really believe Jesus is Lord, and that thought makes me feel good inside." Peter is saying that our faith is reasonable. And that reason is Jesus and all He did for us.

• *The hope that you have.* This means our unsaved friends have noticed something more hopeful about us. By the way we have lived and by our words, we have given evidence of a quality of life, a reason for living, a hope. Most people don't have much hope. They're just trying to survive from day to day. But we have hope in Christ, and that hope is an anchor that keeps us from being swept away by life's storms (Hebrews 6:19). People are curious about and thirsty for what we have.

There may be other key words your group observes in I Peter 3:15 (set apart, Lord, gentleness, respect), but it all boils down to this: As a disciple, Christ has called believers to make disciples, and the only way we can do that is if we know how to communicate our faith.

 Discuss some of Jesus' everyday witnessing opportunities listed under question three in Section III of the disciple's journal on page 131. Point out that Jesus never told His disciples to do witnessing, but rather to be witnesses for Him. In other words, sharing Christ should be an overflow of our relationship with Him, not a duty. All we need to do is put Jesus first in our lives and then just be real with people. Of course, there is a time to go out and witness. But most of our life is spent doing ordinary, everyday things. So do like Jesus did and use natural life situations to introduce others to God's love.

Direct your group's attention to the examples listed in the journal. Notice how Jesus and His disciples used these circumstances as witnessing tools.

Have everyone look at the list of conversational topics listed on page 132 in the journal. Find out if anyone has actually moved a conversation from one of these topics to the Gospel. Brainstorm how one could smoothly do that with some of the topics.

Reflect and Respond

Most of the people in the group may have been won to Christ by a single individual. Take a quick survey among your group members to find out if this is true.

How many of you came to Christ through the witness of another person (as opposed to a large meeting, camp meeting, revival, on your own, etc.)?

Perhaps many of them were won to the Lord by other people—people who cared enough to lead them to Jesus. People really don't care how much you know until they know how much you care.

Review Jesus' encounter with a leper (Mark 1:40-45) to find out just what it means to care for someone else.

What Jesus Felt—According to Mark, Jesus was filled with compassion for the leper. This phrase literally means that His insides were moved. In other words, when Jesus saw this man's condition—leprosy was a picture of sin—He began to care so deeply about him that He literally felt it in His stomach! To have compassion on someone means that you are affected by their condition.

How does the lost condition of your family members or friends make you feel? Encourage a number of people to talk about their feelings for unsaved people in their lives.

What Jesus Did—Jesus touched the leper. And what made this so amazing was that leprosy was thought to be contagious through touch in that day. The crowd around Jesus must have let out an enormous gasp the moment He touched the leper. Jesus wanted that man to know He loved him. He did something visible, tangible, and memorable for that man that communicated His care.

What can you do for your lost friends to show them you really care? Make sure people give specific, not vague, ideas.

What Jesus Said—Jesus simply said, "I am willing." To an unloved, ostracized, feared, outcast like the leper, these must have been words of hope, love, and understanding. With these words, Jesus brought healing to the leper's broken, hopeless life. We can do something similar for the unsaved people in our lives by speaking the words of hope found in the Good News of Jesus Christ. For someone to be saved, that person must hear the words of the Gospel. So our mouths need to communicate the love of God to our "leprous" world.

Who is God calling you to speak the hope of the Gospel to? They can refer to names written in their journal. They can give first names or merely identify the people by relationship such as friend, relative, neighbor, etc. Find out what approach group members think is needed with each unsaved individual. Have group members break up into pairs in order to share this information on a personal level.

To care, we must feel what Jesus felt for the lost, do what Jesus did for the lost, and say what Jesus said to the lost. We must dare to care as He did.

Jesus' compassion said, "I care."

His touch said, "I understand."

His words said, "I'm willing."

3 Sharing and Prayer

Summarize this week's study in this way:

1. Don't let fear prevent you from being a witness for Christ.

2. Untie your tongue by knowing the Gospel and the reasons for your faith and . . .

3. Dare to demonstrate the love of Christ to others by how you feel, what you do, and what you say.

Finish your time by taking turns praying for the unsaved people on your lists and asking God for opportunities to reach them for Christ soon. Follow up on them to see how they are doing on this. Offer your help and encouragement. Remind group members to always be learners of Christ, followers of Him, and those who share Him with others.

Consider giving people in the group something to remind them of this series (a cross, bookmark, T-shirt, personal note, etc.). Then be sure to tell them how much you love and appreciate them!

And don't forget—live like a disciple, never turn back, and always keep the main thing *The Main Thing!*